# BUILDING RESILIENCE

When There's No Going Back
to the Way Things Were

T0125713

# BUILDING RESILIENCE

## When There's No Going Back to the Way Things Were

Alice Updike Scannell

*Foreword by Stephanie Spellers*

**Morehouse Publishing**
NEW YORK

This book is dedicated to my sister-in-law and my brother
Lillian Sturgis Updike and Edwin Hoyt Updike II
who as individuals and as partners in more than six decades
of marriage are exemplars of radical resilience.

———————

The *Question Thinking™* and *Judger/Learner* mindset information in Chapter 5 is reprinted with permission of the publisher from *Change Your Questions, Change Your Life: 10 Powerful Tools for Life and Work* (2nd ed.), © 2009 by Marilee Adams, Berrett-Koehler Publishers, Inc., San Francisco, CA. All rights reserved.

Photograph on page xii by Alice Updike Scannell

Morehouse Publishing, 19 East 34th Street, New York, NY 10016
Morehouse Publishing is an imprint of Church Publishing Incorporated.
www.churchpublishing.org

Cover design by Jennifer Kopec, 2Pug Design
Typeset by Rose Design

Library of Congress Cataloging-in-Publication Data

A record of this book is available from the Library of Congress.

ISBN-13: 978-1-64065-376-4 (paperback)
ISBN-13: 978-1-64065-377-1 (ebook)

# Contents

# Foreword

A few years ago, I traveled home to Kentucky to lead a Women's Day luncheon at my mom's Baptist church. It was just a few months after the killing of Philando Castile, an innocent black man murdered by police in St. Paul, Minnesota. The whole trip I was wracked with nerves. What could I say to a room full of black women in their sixties and seventies, many of whom had known me since I was in diapers? What word would resonate with a community of elders experiencing fresh trauma and deep frustration?

God gave me one word: "resilience." Rather than preach, I invited the women into a time of reflection on the histories and stories of our resilient mentors and ancestors. We cast back to our African forebears, the men and women captured centuries ago and forced to march on foot for hundreds of miles to the western coast of Ghana, where they were herded into slave forts worse than most prisons. Then they were stacked into ships like cargo. Some survived the deadly months-long Middle Passage across the Atlantic; some did not. Those who lived went on to endure the terror and dehumanization of slavery. Their children lived, created, and struggled through Jim Crow, poverty and disenfranchisement, racism and sexism, the War on Drugs, and mass incarceration.

As our sharing concluded, I summed up what the group already knew: "It takes resilience to resist the forces that would harm the beloved children of God," I said. "But I'm not worried, because I know we've got it. We wouldn't be here today without it. Our ancestors were among the most resilient people to ever walk this planet, and that power lives in us."

It's true for people of African descent, and for indigenous peoples who crossed America on foot with tears in their eyes and backs unbowed. It's true for immigrant families who cross deserts and mountains into America only to be shoved into detention centers.

It's also true for any number of people who have suffered a host of life-altering experiences and demonstrate a hope and strength that makes no sense given all that they have seen. These resilient people didn't just bounce back from pain and loss. They rose up, more creative and flexible, more spiritual and mindful, more courageous and wise, and they embraced new realities with what can only be described as grace. If we learn from them, we become more resilient too.

I didn't discover Alice Updike Scannell's term for this phenomenon—"radical resilience"—until recently, but from the first page of this book, I instinctively recognized the practice. It did not matter that Scannell studied resilience in people who reckoned with adversity and loss related to age, physical disability, and illness. The lessons are universal.

The wisdom of radical resilience is even more vital given this moment in our common life. While I write these words, America is gripped by twin pandemics: COVID-19 and systemic racism. Both have the power to take and crush the lives of entire communities. Both have proved durable in the face of government intervention. Healing both depends on relationship and mutuality, since even people who appear to be "ok" may still be carriers of a disease that means death to others.

The COVID pandemic has left us exiled from our sacred spaces and sacraments, just when we most need tangible, spiritual sustenance. The racial reckoning in the wake of George Floyd's murder has stripped away the innocence of Americans who thought certain horrors could no longer occur in the land of the free and the home of the brave.

Though these are early days for both pandemics, they appear to have the power to reshape at least some of the fundamentals of how we understand being church and living in community. People are asking, "What do we do if we can't go back? And would we even want to go back if we could? Who are we in this new reality?"

Though she passed away in 2019, Alice Scannell's guiding words are uniquely attuned to just this moment. She had already captured the stories, done the research, engaged in sustained and systematic reflection. She knew the difference between bouncing back from hard times and getting on with your life *and* radical resilience, which is so much more profound. Radical resilience is what you exhibit when your life takes a radical turn and there's no going back to the way you've understood yourself and your surroundings, and you find a way to not only survive but also thrive.

Scannell offers winsome tales and practical steps for developing the ten "skills" we need to cultivate if we seek to be resilient. Those skills are mindfulness, courage, perseverance, flexibility, reframing, creativity, realistic optimism, hope, physical activity, and spirituality. Each skill relies on other skills to come to full flower—if I can become more flexible and creative, I will find it easier to experience realistic optimism in a situation where I might otherwise be hopelessly stuck.

Each skill is also best practiced with a supportive community gathered around. I picture the circle of women at Mama's Baptist church. I picture small groups in Episcopal churches in urban centers and farm towns. I picture Twelve-Step groups gathered in basements and on Zoom. I picture protest movement organizations. Resilience-building communities take so many forms. The point is to find one.

When you do, I hope someone like Alice Scannell is in the room: a wise elder who understands radical resilience because she has made it her life's work, a generous spirit who helps to nurture mindfulness, courage, flexibility, hope, and deep spirituality in you. Whether you face a global pandemic, systemic oppression, social upheaval, or a devastating loss that is yours alone, you can learn to rise up. We all can, because that power lives in us all.

The Rev. Canon Stephanie Spellers
Canon to the Presiding Bishop for Evangelism,
Reconciliation, and Creation Care
June 2020

# An Introduction to the Rev. Dr. Alice Beekman Updike Scannell

We (our two sons, Stephen and Andrew, and good friend Mary Myers join me in this) remember Alice for her gifts of presence and empathy, of kindness, love, and compassion. All these strengths, as well as her wisdom, are reflected in her writing. We hope you find her book helpful in your own journey toward greater meaning and fullness of life as you build resilience.

Alice was generous and thoughtful, able to assess people's needs and effectively meet them. She was known for being able to express her opinions but did not expect others necessarily to agree with her. She was honest and forthright, persistent and vigilant. A friend reflected, "Alice had an ability to show strength in the most gentle of ways."

She was a gerontologist, researcher, educator, musician, author, and Episcopal priest. The Rev. Dr. Alice Scannell was born Alice Beekman Updike in 1938 in New York City. She graduated with a music degree from Smith College, received a master's degree in religious education from Union Theological Seminary in New York, and a doctoral degree in gerontology from the School of Urban Studies and Public Affairs, Portland State University.

For the last thirty-five years, gerontology was Alice's passion. "I began to see late life issues as something we had to look at in new ways," she wrote. Inspired by her initial interviews with people facing life-threatening disease and chronic illness, issues of aging and Alzheimer disease, and as she supported individuals through the challenges of illness, cognitive decline, and death as an Episcopal priest and chaplain, her mission became one of enhancing meaning and quality of life, especially for those facing life's greatest challenges. She focused her study, research, and papers on issues related to aging, long-term care, and caregiving. It was that work which led her to the insights on building the skills of resilience that fill this book.

In retirement, Alice and I served as chaplains, supporting retired diocesan clergy and their families. In our own retirement community, Alice became a member of the health and wellness committee. She promoted new ideas and approaches in identifying and addressing the needs of residents with dementia and their caregivers. A care team formed to implement her vision was christened "The Alice Project," in her honor.

As Alice approached her death, she was able to say that her life was fulfilled, that she had been able to accomplish all she had wanted to do. She believed in being actively engaged, which she was until her death in December 2019.

A friend who knew Alice from her Smith College days onwards sent her a greeting card when Alice was being presented for ordination in 1998. The message seems to me to capture Alice's spirit:

> *Those who say it cannot be done*
> *Should not interrupt the person doing it.*

John S. Scannell
Portland, Oregon
Spring 2020

# Introduction

When I took the plunge to change careers in my for-ties, I enrolled in the urban studies doctoral program at Portland State University in Portland, Oregon. I had enjoyed two decades as a music teacher, organist, and choral director, but I felt a growing desire to do something very different. Soon into my course of study, I found that I loved research.

I applied for a research assistant position and was hired to interview midlife and older adults about their experiences with life-threatening diseases or chronic illness. The purpose of the studies was to learn how the respondents' illness affected their social network, psychological well-being, and other important aspects of their lives. Using a structured interview, I talked with people who had experienced stroke, heart failure, emphysema, cancer, and other illnesses that have long-term, life-changing effects. I met with the respondents twice and sometimes three times, several months apart. Through these conversations I became fascinated with the different ways people managed to cope with—and adapt to (or not)—the adversities that had brought life-changing limitations into their lives.

For the next fifteen years, I worked with older adults, first in the university setting and later as a planner, program development specialist, and research consultant for the county's aging and disability services department. I continued to do research on family decision-making in later life and on the challenges of adapting to life in an assisted care community or nursing home. During that time I prepared for ordination as a priest in the Episcopal Church. I began my service as a priest by developing a spiritual care program to serve residents, families, and staff at an assisted living community for people with Alzheimer disease and related disorders.

The idea for this book came in response to a comment I overheard one evening while I was waiting in line at a symphony concert. As two older women were catching up with each other, one said to the other, "Nobody ever prepares you for growing old." I envisioned writing a book that would help us prepare to meet the challenges of later life. Resilience was to be the subject of the first chapter. However, as I studied the published research on adult resilience and reflected on what I'd learned from my own research, I realized that I wanted to first write a book about resilience itself. I wanted to show, from research-based evidence as well as from my experience and those of others who have shared their stories, how we can develop the capacity for the kind of resilience that empowers us, at any age, to be ourselves when our lives change or when we can no longer do the things we used to do that gave our lives satisfaction, meaning, and purpose.

There are now many books about resilience—about how to *bounce back from* adversities and return to our normal lives. This book is different. It's about *radical* resilience—the kind of resilience we need, not to bounce back from, but to *work through* the adversities that change our lives, the adversities that deliver a *new* reality in which we must make a new life. Developing the capacity to be radically resilient when we can no longer do what we used to involves consciously using skills throughout our lives that help us deal successfully with any kind of change or frustration, including growing old.

Resilience research tells us that resilience is not so much a personality trait as it is the result of our attitudes and behaviors in response to the adverse events in our life.[1] I call these attitudes and behaviors *resilience skills* because when we use them intentionally we get better at them with practice. My objective for this book is to show how we can start at any point in our lives to build our capacity for radical resilience by practicing these skills.

Many of us do the bounce-back kind of resilience pretty well as we handle the changes and challenges of life. But a life-changing adversity can deplete our usual capacity to do what we used to do to be ourselves. We may lose hope of ever being ourselves again. Using some or all of the resilience skills presented here can release us from our despair and help us figure out how to reshape our lives over time so that we retain our sense of self and feel at peace in our new reality.

In this book you'll read stories of real people who illustrate *radical* resilience. They've come through many different life-changing adversities—loss of limbs, death of a spouse, life-threatening and life-changing illnesses, accidental injuries, and others. These stories show how a variety of people have used these resilience skills to get to the other side of hopelessness and despair when adversity threw a curve into their lives. For some, the resilience turnaround came soon after they began to process the reality of their situation. For others, the process of resilience was slower, sometimes taking several years. For most of the resilient people in this book, the effects of their adversity were permanent. For a few, a resolution of the adverse effects was expected to occur within six months to a year. But all faced the fear of not being able to be fully themselves again because of what had happened to them.

Some of the people you'll read about learned to use resilience skills for the first time. Others were challenged to use and expand some skills they hadn't consciously used for many years. Some felt that what they did to overcome their adversity came naturally to them—they wouldn't say that they had used skills to do it. Without realizing it, though, they did employ the strategies that I call resilience skills. They worked hard over many months to reclaim their lives from the adversity that threatened to overwhelm them.

Chapter 1 presents a framework for understanding radical resilience. It shows how our attitudes, choices, and self-image influence our capacity to be resilient and lays the foundation for the later chapters.

Chapters 2–9 present the ten aspects of resilience that I call *resilience skills:* mindfulness, courage, perseverance, flexibility, reframing, creativity (a skill with many more facets than the artistic ones we usually associate with the word), realistic optimism, hope, physical activity, and spirituality. These skills are not only necessary for radical resilience, they are also valuable for our lives now. Practicing them in our daily living will improve our communication, strengthen our relationships, and deepen both our self-awareness and our inner life. As we begin to use these skills regularly in response to any change or conflict, they'll become firmly placed in our life-skills toolbox, ready for use whenever we need them. The *Ways to Practice* sections in each chapter suggest steps we can take to practice the skills that will help us be resilient throughout our life. As we follow the practice suggestions, we'll undoubtedly discover other ways to make these practices our own. We can practice each of the ten skills in any way we wish. They'll enhance our life and help us get through the changes and challenges that are so often part of our life's journey. A summary table for each of the skills is included at the end of their respective chapters.

Chapter 10 describes how radical resilience is a process that takes time—many weeks, often months, and sometimes years. During that process we may experience setbacks, plateaus, and times of pain and discouragement. Radical resilience draws on every capacity we have to move forward emotionally, physically, and spiritually after adversity has changed our life and we can't go back to the way things were. Our aim in working through the process of radical resilience is to reach the state of feeling whole again, ready to live our life with meaning and purpose in our new reality.

Chapter 11 presents resources for further exploration of the themes and skills presented in Chapters 1–10.

My life has been enhanced by writing this book. I hope that reading it and incorporating the skills into your life will enhance yours.

# 1

# Radical Resilience

When my friend LouAnn asked me what this book was about, I told her that it's about resilience—not so much the kind where you rebound from difficulties and get on with your life but the kind when there's no going back to what was before and you have to figure out how to be yourself in that new reality.

"Oh my gosh," she said. "That's huge." She told me that she had surgery on her neck about a year before and some of the nerves to her tongue were bruised. For several months she couldn't move her tongue enough to talk or chew food. "I'm a storyteller," she said, with a tone of alarm in her voice. "What was I going to do? I couldn't be myself. It was a terrible time. If I'd thought it would be a permanent condition, I really don't know what I would have done. It would have felt like I could never really be *me* again."

We usually think of resilience as the ability to recover from an adverse experience and pick up our lives where we left off. It is that too. LouAnn was fortunate that her tongue muscles eventually recovered. But there are times when adversity permanently changes our reality and we can't go back to the way things were. We can't do the things we used to do that were part of our identity—the things that gave meaning and purpose to our lives, that gave us a reason to live. It feels as though our quality of life has been smashed to pieces and is gone forever. Fear for our future wrenches our insides. We don't know what we'll do.

When adversity permanently changes our reality, there is no going back to the way things were. Resilience then becomes the work of *coming through* the adversity so that, at least on most days, we see our life as still worth living. With this kind of resilience, we come through the adversity knowing that we're still ourselves, even though things are very different for us now. I call this *radical* resilience.

Jan Schumacher is an example of radical resilience.[1] She was the owner of a high-end bridal shop before a blood infection nearly killed her. In the painful and lengthy process of treatment and recovery, Schumacher lost parts of both thumbs and all or parts of her fingers on both hands. "But I really got a miracle," she said as she held up her hands to show her prosthetic appendages. The prosthetics didn't look much like hands. They looked more like the claws of a lobster or a crab. But they gave her the ability to grasp, to pick up and hold things—something she hadn't been able to do for months. They felt like a gift. For Schumacher, they're a miracle.

After almost a year, she was ready to move on to the next chapter of her life. She exuded vitality as she wondered what she would do next. However, she didn't think it would be the person-to-person sales she loves. Those sales are usually sealed with a handshake, which she thought would be awkward for her customers. Schumacher was certain that she wanted to do something that would help others. And because she loved running her own business, she wanted whatever she decided on to be something that she could still do herself.

Radical resilience is a challenge. It's *radical* because it connects with the roots of our being. Radical resilience draws from our essential self, demanding that we engage with meaning and hope in new ways in order to feel that our life is still worth living. It's radical also because it's accompanied at some point by a surprising sense of gratitude, as Jan showed as she held up her awkward mechanical hands and called them her *miracle*. And it's radical because it transforms us, both inwardly and outwardly. We learn that wholeness is a state of being, that life can have meaning and purpose under many different circumstances.

Unlike Jan Schumacher, Virginia wasn't able to engage the skills of radical resilience after she fell and broke her hip. Virginia was my first boss right after my college graduation. She was the director of education in a large, urban congregation and she loved her job. She was my mentor during a one-year apprenticeship program before I started my seminary training to be a lay director of religious education. A widow in her mid-fifties, Virginia had abundant energy and enthusiasm for life. She not only had a friendly and engaging personality, she seemed like a human dynamo. She moved fast, talked fast, and could do more visits in a day than anyone else on the staff. People of all ages, including me, loved and admired her.

For many years I thought of Virginia as a model of resilience. She simply refused to be held down by any adversity that came her way. When one senior living arrangement didn't work out the way she expected it to, she left and found a different one. When her shoulder became a problem, she had surgery to fix it and was back to her former activities in record time. She handled other challenges the same way, always getting back to where she'd left off. Yet in retrospect, I see now that Virginia never learned how to *move through those challenges* toward a deeper understanding of herself. She didn't look for meaning in her new realities; instead, she refused to live in them, and she endured the passage of time in recovery or discontent as best she could until she could get back to living life as she used to. Then she broke her hip.

I visited Virginia several years ago when I was in her city for a meeting. Although we'd corresponded through occasional letters, I hadn't seen her in more than ten years. She was living in the same retirement community as on my last visit, though she now had a live-in caregiver who greeted me at the door. Virginia reclined on the sofa the whole time of my visit. A walker was visible across the room but not handy for immediate use. It seems that Virginia hated to use the walker, and so she did as little walking as possible.

Soon into our conversation, I learned that several months into recovery from hip surgery, when Virginia didn't get back on her feet as easily as before, she realized that she probably would never move as well as she wanted to. So she stopped going anywhere at all. She wouldn't leave her apartment except for medical appointments. Rather than go to the dining room for meals, she paid extra for meals to be brought to her apartment. She didn't want to go to any of the interesting lectures or discussion groups that she'd previously loved. I was surprised and asked why she didn't want to do those things anymore.

"I'm not depressed," she told me vehemently. "This is just not the way I want to be seen."

A number of years before, I'd learned that Virginia had been very pleased and proud to be part of a long-term research study on aging. In this study, participants were interviewed every few years from the time they joined the study, around age fifty, through to the end of their lives.[2] Over the years, Virginia had enthusiastically told me about going for the study interviews and about the various brainteaser tests and other measures that were part of the data collection. So I asked her about it.

"Oh, I dropped out," she said.

"You dropped out?" I said. "I thought the purpose of the study was to learn about what real aging is like for real people, from the time you're in until you die."

"I know," Virginia said, "but I'm not good at getting old, so I decided to drop out."

As our conversation continued, I mentioned to her that she was still able to think well and that she still had her ready wit and sense of humor. She smiled and said she was glad I thought so. I asked her to think about going to an occasional lecture or discussion group in her building because it would be invigorating and give her back some energy. I even encouraged her to consider getting back into the study so she could express honestly how she felt about her experience with aging. But she wasn't interested in talking further about any of these things. We spent the rest of our time together sharing memories of the past.

I left the visit sad and discouraged. Virginia had always been my model for resilience, and suddenly she was not. I wonder now if that experience wasn't my first awareness that there's a different kind of resilience than the bounce-back kind, the kind of resilience that gets us through not being able to do what we used to do—the *radical* resilience that empowers us to find meaning and purpose in our lives when our life's journey takes a new turn, and our familiar ways of being and doing suddenly become obsolete.

## Ten Skills for Radical Resilience

My research helped me develop the list of ten aspects of resilience that I call *resilience skills*: mindfulness, courage, perseverance, flexibility, reframing, creativity, realistic optimism, hope, physical activity, and spirituality.

Why do I call them "*skills*"? Because it takes awareness, intentionality, and practice to develop them. Other people might call them practices or attitudes, but I prefer to call them skills because we get better at them as we apply them. Alone or in combination, these ten skills, when used intentionally to respond to any kind of change, open up the path to resilience by helping us to see and do things differently. They are important skills that are useful in many settings—so important, in fact, that I've seen them in many business books on management and leadership.[3]

Whenever we're challenged by change in our daily lives, we can intentionally practice a resilience skill. When we're anxious or distracted, we can center ourselves by practicing mindfulness. When we come upon a detour or need to adjust to a sudden change in plans, we can neutralize our frustration by choosing to see these as opportunities to practice flexibility. As we learn how each of the skills can strengthen our capacity for resilience, we'll become aware of abundant opportunities to practice the skills that hone our capacity to be radically resilient.

I've engaged these skills often as I've been writing this book. My own experience concurs with evidence from research—these skills help enormously to move us out from a place of despair, frustration, and loss into a more fruitful place of centeredness and inner strength. They help us let go of the past. Moreover, they help us move forward, with hope and a sense of self, into the future.

## Five Important Conditions for Radical Resilience

To make the best use of the ten resilience skills, there are some other things we'll want to focus on. These are self-awareness, supportive relationships, openness, reflection, and humor.

**Self-awareness.** It's important that we stay in touch with—and expand if we need to—our capacity for self-awareness. In order to respond with resilience to changes in our lives, especially the changes that require radical resilience, we must be able to face the truths (both positive and negative) about ourselves and see ourselves as others see us. This includes awareness of our attitudes that are judgmental or biased, awareness of how well we communicate with others, and awareness of how well we listen.

It also includes awareness of experiences in our lives that might influence how we interpret situations, how we behave in response to confrontation or criticism, how we view people who are different from us, and how we handle disappointment and loss. All of these, unless acknowledged and understood, may limit our capacity to engage in the work of radical resilience.

**Supportive relationships.** It's hard to do the work of radical resilience alone. Whatever the circumstances of our adversity, we'll do much better if we have people to whom we can talk, with whom we can share our thoughts, and from whom we can request specific assistance or support. Sometimes the people who serve in those roles are not our closest friends or family members. Often they'll be professionals who have specific training to help us come through our adversity. Or they may be organizations and support groups specifically formed to help people who have experienced similar adversities. It's important to avoid isolation and to find acceptance through a group or a trusted confidante. Having at least one trusted person with whom we can share our deepest concerns and with whom we can be completely honest is central to our sense of well-being not only when we're recovering from adversity, but also throughout our life. That person may be a counselor or a spiritual leader. Or he or she may be a close friend and confidante.

**Openness.** Openness is being willing to hear honest feedback from people we trust. However, openness also includes being willing to express our thoughts, feelings, doubts, fears, and truths to those people or others we trust. Sharing the stories we're ashamed to tell about ourselves with someone who will accept us as we are, respect our stories, and hold our stories in confidence liberates us from the bonds of secrecy and embarrassment. Sharing our stories with trusted others is a step forward in the healing process of radical resilience.

**Reflection.** This is the capacity to think about our experiences and learn from them. Reflection is not simply going over and over an experience in our minds. Rather, it is contemplating the experience in order to gain insight from it. Reflection includes naming the emotions we felt before, during, and after the experience, and asking ourselves what the experience has to teach us. Sometimes reflecting on a current experience will call to mind an experience from the past that links to it, leading us to a deeper understanding of ourselves and how we process some of the things that happen to us. Insights that result from reflection broaden our awareness not only of ourselves but of possibilities, and they help us to see multiple ways that we can understand or do things differently.

**Humor.** A gentle sense of humor and an ability to take ourselves lightly when we are stressed increase our capacity for radical resilience. Both gentle laughter and spontaneous guffaws help dissolve inner tension. They help us relax, and that in itself can give us a refreshed perspective on life. Years ago, when I was hospitalized for several weeks with severe back pain and pregnancy complications, a friend brought me books that made me laugh in spite of myself. This surprised and confused my elderly roommate, who asked me, "How can you laugh when you hurt so much?"

I was surprised by her question. "Because this is really funny," I said. I was very glad to have something lighthearted that drew me into a different world and took my mind off my pain.

## Moving Forward

When change strikes us hard and there is no going back to what was before, self-awareness, supportive relationships, openness, the ability to reflect and to learn from our experience, and a sense of humor become a framework for our capacity to respond to life's changes with *radical* resilience.

The people and stories of resilience here continue to inspire and encourage me. From them, and from my own experience using these resilience skills, I've learned that we don't have to lose hope when we find ourselves in an undesirable new reality. We don't have to despair when limitations cut us off from doing the things we love to do, the things that give us energy, that help us be ourselves, that give us a sense of meaning and purpose in our lives. Resilience skills bring us to a place where we can see a positive future for ourselves even in a different, unplanned reality. Resilience skills teach us how to explore ways to create that future. Practicing them as we respond to changes and challenges in our daily life makes them readily available to us when we face the challenges of adversity and the challenges of growing old.

Although the resilience skills work together well, they are also independent. We can start practicing them in any order to build or strengthen our capacity for resilience. May the following chapters be a catalyst and a guide to move you forward toward building your own set of radical resilience skills.

## Summary for Chapter 1: Radical Resilience

What is radical resilience? Skills needed to *work through, rather than bounce back from,* life-changing adversities.

What are the radical resilience skills? Mindfulness, courage, perseverance, flexibility, reframing, creativity, realistic optimism, hope, physical activity, and spirituality.

What often characterizes the radical resilience process? As we come through adversity into a new sense of self and well-being in our new reality, it is normal to experience setbacks, plateaus, and times of discouragement. The ten skills help us get through these times too.

What qualities support the radical resilience process? Self-awareness, supportive relationships, openness, the ability to reflect on our experience, and a sense of humor.

Who needs radical resilience skills? We all do. The sooner we build the skills into our daily lives, the greater capacity we'll have to handle change of any kind, including the difficult changes that come from adverse happenings in our lives.

# 2

# Mindfulness

indfulness is the practice of being attentive and aware. I call it a resilience skill because it clears away our inclination to respond habitually or reactively when we're confronted with troublesome situations. As with other skills, the more we do it, the better we get at it. When we consciously move into mindfulness, we create a space inside us that frees us from mental and emotional distractions. Mindfulness works by interrupting our automatic, habit-based responses. It releases us from the grip of reaction. It calms and centers us. It prepares us to respond to tense or frustrating situations with thoughtful, open-minded awareness. When we practice mindfulness, we unhook our attention from mental stewing and turn it toward our breathing. This simple action of paying attention to our breath—slowly breathing in, then slowly breathing out—centers and grounds us.

Mindfulness practice brings us into the present moment. It creates a mental and emotional space—a breathing space—for us to change course from a reactive frame of mind to an alert, aware frame of mind. We're then able to respond with non-judgmental observation to the realities of the present moment. We can then make a clear-headed choice about how to proceed.

The opposite of mindfulness is mindlessness. Mindlessness is acting automatically, unaware of how a situation could be *different this time.* When we're mindless, we tend to jump to conclusions and react, often missing something important that we should have noticed. A tragic example of this is the fatal crash of Air Florida flight 90 as it took off from Washington, DC's National Airport in January 1982. The National Transportation Safety Board found that a probable cause of the crash was that the engine's anti-icer was in the "off" position, both before and during takeoff. The evidence showed that the anti-icer had never been turned on, even while the plane waited on the tarmac in snowy, icy weather.[1]

Why wasn't the anti-icer turned on during the pilots' checklist process? Why did neither the pilot nor the co-pilot realize that in this weather the engine's anti-icer should be on? Mindfulness expert Ellen Langer posits that the fatal mistake was made because in the pilots' previous experience with this flight, the correct position for the anti-icer had always been *off.*[2] These two pilots were used to flying back and forth to Florida when there had never been a need for the anti-icer to be on. Most likely, wanting to get the plane on its way after being delayed, the pilot and copilot went through the checklist without thinking about how *this time was different.* Because they weren't mindfully aware that the unusually cold weather would affect the plane, they missed the fact *that for this flight* the position of the anti-icer should be on. As a result, the plane crashed into the 14th Street Bridge, and seventy-nine people, including four members of the crew, lost their lives.[3]

Most of us can think of instances of mindlessness in our own lives. Fortunately, most of our mindless actions don't have harmful consequences, like missing a turn when we're driving because we're thinking about something else. Or losing our car in a parking garage because we walk away without noticing what section we parked in. Or throwing the wrong papers in the recycle bin because we're in a hurry and we aren't paying attention when we gather them up and toss them in. Unless we cultivate our capacity for mindfulness, we can easily fall into the habitual, automatic behaviors that are trademarks of mindlessness: thinking about something else, not noticing our surroundings, not paying attention when we do regular or habitual actions.

In contrast to mindlessness, with its quality of automatic response, mindfulness is being awake and aware, observant of the reality of the present moment without assumptions or bias. The practice of mindfulness can range from consciously and holisti-cally attending to how we live our lives as a whole person—body, mind, heart, and spirit—to a variety of meditation practices. The action of intentionally interrupting an automatic response and shifting our attention to our breath for a couple of minutes can be enough to move us into an attitude of mindfulness. Other mindfulness practices include sitting meditation, walking medi-tation, mindfulness-based stress reduction programs, and mind-body-movement practices such as tai chi and yoga.

## Mindfulness as a Holistic Approach to Life

We can begin mindfulness practice by consciously attending to how we're living our lives as a whole person. This is the least formal approach to mindfulness practice. It focuses on understanding our values, hopes, and dreams; assessing our life to see how we're living in relation to them; and making choices that sustain our sense of meaning and purpose in life.[4]

People who lead mindful lives in this way may never practice formal mindfulness meditation; however, they do practice self-awareness, pay attention to wake-up calls, and learn from experience. In essence, they have a mindful approach to life—they keep themselves awake, aware, and learning.

When I think of this approach to mindfulness, I think of Bob. His story shows how mindfulness can guide us as we evaluate our reality, envision possibilities, and choose actions that move us forward.

When Bob was in his forties, he decided to be consciously attentive to three important areas of his life: his relationship to his work, to his family, and to the dreams he'd once had for his life. He'd always wanted to work outdoors, be close to nature, and grow his own food. In fact, when he was young, he'd wanted to be a farmer. But his life had taken a very different, though satisfying, direction. He ended up as a surgeon.

Bob's mindful attention to his life led him to buy a small farm out in the country about an hour from his home. Since he wanted to continue full-time with his medical practice, he hired a helper to live on the property and tend to the few head of cattle that he'd purchased. As the years flew by, Bob went to his farm at least weekly, when possible, to share in the work and decisions.

Around the time of his sixtieth birthday, Bob realized that advances in medical technology were requiring that physicians and surgeons learn new methods and procedures to treat their patients. Bob could see that he would soon need further training to keep up with the rapid changes in his field. Being mindful that decisions about his professional life were on the horizon, he decided to assess how he was doing in relation to his values, hopes, and dreams.

Bob had loved his work as a physician. Yet he'd also loved the time he spent on his farm. He still yearned to be a farmer full-time, working outside, tending the land, cultivating a garden, and raising some more animals. During his mindful assessment of his life as a whole person, Bob realized that if he was going to farm, he wanted to do it while he was still physically strong enough to do most of the work himself. So at sixty-two, he took an early retirement from his medical practice.

Soon after his retirement Bob and his wife took a road trip. While on this trip they discovered a lovely farm property for sale. It was near a college town, and though it was in a different state, they both felt that this was the place where they'd like to settle. They bought the property and moved within a few months. Bob soon acquired some sheep, some goats, a few cows, and a variety of organic fruit trees. He developed a large organic garden, and for the next twenty-five years, he and his wife enjoyed their life on their beautiful and productive land.

Bob remained alert to the realities of life as he and his wife grew older. When a new senior retirement community was built near the college, the management offered local people an option to make a fully refundable deposit that would keep them on a waiting list until such time as they might need to make a move. In addition, people who made a deposit would qualify for temporary stays there if they needed to be in town and close to their doctors between a hospitalization and going home. Mindful of the realities of aging, Bob made the deposit. He considered it a good investment in peace of mind should he or his wife ever need temporary assistance or if the time should come when their farm home no longer met their needs. In addition, he liked the assurance that if they never moved there, he'd get his money back.

Bob's mindful approach to life enhanced his life in many ways. It increased his self-awareness and gave him the courage to try many new things that he thought he would enjoy. He was invited to use his farm to teach groups of young people about organic gardening and soil conservation. He served on the board of the state's permaculture group and participated in developing a curriculum to teach permaculture and soil conservation in high schools. He learned to shear his sheep, card the wool, spin the yarn, and weave. In addition, Bob learned to play the banjo and the bass fiddle well enough to play in the weekly jam sessions at the local music store.

Now approaching ninety, Bob continues to be mindful. He and his wife are again in transition. They recently moved to the retirement community and are discerning ways they can each keep active and engaged in meaningful and fulfilling pursuits. Being mindful has helped Bob become who he is. It's likely that his mindful approach to life will serve him well as he continues to explore ways to respond to his life's realities with creativity and courage.

## Mindfulness Meditation

The more formal approaches to becoming mindful are rooted in the practice of mindfulness meditation. Though this may sound intimidating, it isn't. As I've mentioned before, just intentionally interrupting an automatic response and shifting our attention to our breath for a couple of minutes is enough to move us into an attitude of mindfulness. When we focus on our breathing and gradually release the tension in our bodies, we disengage from what's bothering us. A sense of calm takes its place, empowering us to observe our situation without reaction or judgment.

For example, not long ago I had a follow-up phone conversation that made me very angry. Several days previously I had called a health insurance customer advocate about a concern. I had explained my situation clearly and answered all his questions. At his request, I also faxed a follow-up letter to him detailing what we had discussed on the phone. He said he would call me back with information about the next steps I should take to resolve the problem.

A few minutes into his follow-up call several days later, I realized that he hadn't understood my situation at all. He kept asking questions that I'd already answered in both the previous phone conversation and the faxed letter that fully documented the issue. Suddenly, I was furious. After all my efforts to establish good communication about my concern, he had absolutely no understanding of it. I tried to remain civil as I brought the conversation to a hasty close.

Fuming and frustrated, I remembered mindfulness practice. I realized that playing the conversation over and over in my mind was not a mindful approach. I sat down and began to pay attention to my breathing. Shallow and rapid at first, it soon became slow and steady. In just a few minutes I felt calm and centered. My feelings of anger and frustration dissolved as I focused my attention on my breathing and gradually released the physical tensions that built up during the conversation.

I remembered that mindfulness practice would have me consider the conversation from the standpoint of an observer, noticing what was said by each of us in a neutral way, without reacting or judging. I felt calm and objective as I noted the reality that he hadn't understood my situation. My reactive emotions did not recur as I reviewed the conversation from a mindfulness perspective. I saw that I'd done all I could with this approach to solving my problem; I didn't need to deal with that office again. The thought came to me that there were a few other avenues I could pursue. I decided to let go of thinking about this for a while. Then, as I started to move on to other things, the name of a friend who had experience with the issue I was trying to solve came into my mind. I couldn't believe it. I wondered why I hadn't thought of this person weeks before when I started to work on solving the issue. Receiving that name felt like receiving a gift—I knew this person would point me in the right direction. So, within moments of ending the frustrating call and initiating a short time of mindfulness meditation, I felt restored and at peace.

I learned a lot from this experience of mindfulness meditation. Not only did I get a broader perspective on how to resolve my situation, I also experienced how mindfulness meditation releases us from the power of negative emotions. Even as I've continued to pursue a solution to my situation and have talked with several people since the time of the problematic phone conversation, I've never felt a return of anger or frustration.

Occasions of intentional mindfulness can act as a reset button. They break into our ruminative thinking and create a space for us to step back mentally and emotionally from what bothers us. Running a conversation or incident over and over again in our minds is not helpful—it only increases our inner tension. Intentional mindfulness is the action of stepping back from what bothers us to gain a calm and accepting perspective, without bias or assumptions, on the reality of the present moment. In her book *Ten Thousand Joys and Ten Thousand Sorrows*, Olivia Hoblitzelle tells how she drew on mindfulness practice when she became a caregiver for her husband, Hob, as Alzheimer disease gradually deconstructed his life.[5]

As Hob's disease progressed, he lost the capacity to remember things. He couldn't remember where he put things he needed. If Olivia was out, he couldn't remember when she'd be home. As with others who experience this devastating disease, Hob's pent-up anxiety about the things he couldn't remember would often be expressed in behaviors that were intense and sometimes frightening.

"After a series of unnerving episodes," she writes, "I evolved a ritual for coming home even if I'd been away for only a few hours. . . . Each time I arrived home, in those moments between leaving the car, stepping onto the old brick walk, and entering the house, I shifted into mindfulness practice: walking and breathing mindfully, aware of each step, each breath. Just before the door, I repeated a simple *metta*, or loving-kindness prayer. That was how I steadied myself in preparation for the inevitable—the latest crisis waiting for me on the other side of the door."[6]

Hoblitzelle named these moments of mindfulness her *pathway practice*. This pathway practice softened the shocks of coming home and being immediately approached by Hob in his highly anxious state. It also fortified her patience and allowed her heart to stay open.[7]

Psychologists Daphne Davis and Jeffrey Hayes have synthesized findings from a number of evidence-based research studies that show the many benefits of mindfulness.[8] Among them are reduced rumination, stress reduction, improvements to working memory, less emotional reactivity, more cognitive flexibility, relationship satisfaction, and improved health and well-being.[9] Other studies show that mindfulness-based stress reduction training is a useful intervention for a broad range of chronic disorders and problems such as cancer, low back pain, fibromyalgia, rheumatoid arthritis, cardiovascular disease, diabetes, and others.[10]

## Some Ways to Practice Mindfulness

We can begin simply by building an attitude of mindfulness into our daily routine. This involves consciously paying attention to our surroundings, our senses, and our emotions in the moment—right when they're present. We observe them without judgment, as if we were an interested onlooker. Starting to *notice with awareness* is an excellent first step in learning to be mindful. We can do it anywhere and at any time, while walking, eating, chatting, sitting quietly, or simply going about our daily routine.

We can also begin by responding to incidents that frustrate or anger us with a mindfulness breathing practice. This is what I did in response to the upsetting phone call with the customer advocate. I interrupted my fuming by closing my eyes and taking a few slow, deep breaths. Conscious of the rhythm of my breathing and mentally repeating, *"breathe in . . . center . . . breathe out . . . center,"* I start to release the tension in my body.

I usually begin by relaxing my head, jaw, neck, and shoulders. I continue to be aware of relaxing each part of my body until I feel the tension go out through my toes. Sometimes, though, I'll start by relaxing my feet and legs and moving up and out through the top of my head. After I feel calm and relaxed, and still breathing intentionally, I gently repeat to myself, *"let it be . . . let it go for now . . . let it be."* When I feel ready, I open my eyes and slowly return to awareness of the present moment.

This process doesn't need to take long to have a positive result. Especially if you use it in response to an upsetting episode, it may take only a couple of minutes. However, as a regular practice to increase our ability to be mindfully aware and present in daily life, longer sessions are better.[11]

**After you become familiar with the mindful attitude practice, you may want to try the following mindfulness practice for a week.** Once a day, or more if you like, sit comfortably— or walk at a relaxed pace—for about ten minutes. Notice the time of day, notice how your body feels, get comfortable in your surroundings. If you're outside, notice the color of the sky and the feeling of the weather on your face. Relax. Breathe deeply and slowly, in and out. Feel the rhythm of your breath. At the end of your time, make note of one particular thing to remember about this time of meditation. You might want to write it down so you won't forget it. At the end of the week, reflect on how this practice of meditation affected the quality of your life or your sense of well-being. If you found it hard to remember to do this practice each day, continue with a goal of doing it two or more times a week until the practice feels like a comfortable and natural way to center yourself in the midst of inner or outer busyness.

**If you're ready to continue, try this.** A quiet, peaceful place is an important component of mindfulness practice. You'll also need a chair that supports good posture or a comfortable pillow for floor sitting. It's helpful to set a timer that will give you a gentle tone when the time is up—you'll want to avoid an abrupt ending to your mindfulness practice. Try for 3–4 minutes at first, then 10. Over time, you may want to gradually increase your mindfulness practice time to 30–45 minutes or an hour.

After setting your timer, enter your mindfulness practice time sitting comfortably. Begin to engage your mind and body in deep, regular breathing. Breathe in. Breathe out. Slowly. Deeply. Close your eyes. Empty your mind of thoughts. If thoughts appear (as they often do), let them go. Concentrate on your breathing. Allow your body to relax. Connect with how your body feels. Relax into your breath, your center. Remember that the purpose of this time is to clear your mind and body of tension and distractions, centering them both in quiet consciousness.

Sometimes it's helpful to concentrate on a *mantra*—a word or phrase that is calming and meaningful to you. Be comfortable simply being in the moment. Sometimes you may even nap during this time. That's okay. Self-compassion is an important aspect of mindfulness. When your timer rings, gently come back to awareness of your surroundings.[12]

I've found that brief periods of mindfulness practice are very helpful as a lead-in to intentional engagement with other resilience skills. When I'm tense, fearful, anxious, or experiencing pain, I use a short mindfulness practice to help me calm down and get my bearings. Then I can see more clearly what resilience skills would be best to use to solve the challenge ahead. For example, it might be good if I reframe the situation and try to see it from some other perspectives. Or maybe I need to be flexible. Maybe I need the courage to ask for help. Maybe a walk would help. Or maybe the situation calls for me to practice perseverance—to keep showing up and staying present.

Mindfulness practice sets the stage for the practice of the other nine resilience skills in this book. However, there is much more to mindfulness practice than can be covered in this chapter. Readers who want to go beyond the basics that are presented here will find additional resources at the end of this book.

## Summary for Chapter 2: Mindfulness

### What is mindfulness as a radical resilience skill?

- The practice of being attentive and aware.
- Unhooking our attention from mental stewing and turning it toward our breathing.

### What are the benefits of mindfulness?

- Creates a space inside us free from mental and emotional distractions.
- Calms and centers us.
- Prepares us to respond to tense or frustrating situations with thoughtful, open-minded awareness.

### What are some ways to practice mindfulness?

- Paying attention in the moment of our daily routines—to surroundings, senses, emotions. Simply becoming aware.
- Responding to upsetting episodes with mindfulness breathing:
  - Slowly breathe in, center our attention on our breath, slowly breathe out.
  - Repeat until we feel calm.
- Giving mindful attention to how we are living our life: are our choices, big and small, aligned with our values, hopes, and dreams?

# 3

# Courage
# and Perseverance

Courage and perseverance are fundamental character-istics of radical resilience. They sustain us in the dark times when all we can do is simply be, they undergird our will to live when all seems hopeless, and they empower us to keep on doing the best we can in the midst of pain and uncertainty. Courage is firmness of mind and will in the face of extreme difficulty. Perseverance is the continued effort to do or achieve something despite difficulties, failures, or opposition. I call courage and perseverance "*skills*" because, as with other skills, we get better at them with practice.

The stories of radical resilience are all stories of courage and perseverance. Although each story illustrates one particular resilience skill, you'll notice that other resilience skills are also part of that person's story. No matter how many resilience skills we use in adapting to the effects of adverse events, courage and perseverance are essential components of radical resilience.

Radical resilience is a process as well as an outcome. That's why courage and perseverance are important to it: our recovery, restoration, and adaptation to whatever has created a new and negative reality for our lives takes many months.

Often, the process of resilience takes years. The adversities that call for radical resilience turn our life upside down. They expose our vulnerability. They catapult us into an emotional abyss and force us to face an unknown future. They're accompanied by emotional pain and often by physical pain. Many times they evoke a sense of shame in us, and we don't know why. These are all significant challenges to our deepest sense of self. It takes courage to face them. It also takes perseverance to keep on working to overcome them, especially when the emotional and/or physical work that is required to do so is daunting.

When an adverse event suddenly changes our life, it's normal to experience sadness, depression, fear, and anxiety. Usually some time will pass before we're able to look at our situation and make some conscious choices about how we'll respond. Courage and perseverance play their part as we live with our new reality and begin to face our questions, our feelings, our fears, our doubts, and our hopes. Each step we take toward recovery and restoration, even as we grapple with the intensity of what's going on in our thoughts and feelings, are steps taken with courage. Each time we choose to move forward one little bit, in the face of tremendous pain or uncertainty, we're persevering toward wholeness.

For example, when we try to walk after a stroke, or talk when our tongue muscles don't work and what we say comes out as clear as mud, or exercise when we're depressed, or speak to a counselor when we're awash in shame or guilt, or graciously receive help with intimate personal care, then we're practicing courage. When we keep taking small, courageous steps to keep our sense of self alive in our new and unwelcomed reality, then we're practicing perseverance.

Edith's long recovery after a horrendous car crash that broke her spirit and her body is a story of courage and perseverance. For months after the accident, she was in the depths of despair. Her whole body felt broken. The constant pain from her broken legs, her broken right arm, and several broken vertebrae was unbearable, even after taking the maximum dose of painkillers. She felt no relief from the pain in her body, and no relief from the pain in her soul either.

Edith sometimes wished she had died in the crash. She couldn't see how she could continue living with the tremendous pain. She dreaded the physical therapy sessions that made her feel worse; she shied away from doing exercises at home. Nothing relieved her depression. Then one morning Edith woke up and realized that she had slept through the night without waking up for a pain pill. "I was so grateful," she said. "I felt a glimmer of hope, and I thought to myself, I can do this. I'm going to work as best I can to gradually get better. I may not be able to walk as well as I could before, but I'm going to get back to being myself and living a normal life the best I can."

It took the better part of a year for Edith to recover from the effects of the accident. She had many ups and downs in that process. But she never lost sight of her goal to get her sense of self back and live a normal life. After another year of working toward her recovery, she was able to return to full-time teaching.

Now, several years later, Edith is grateful for the discovery of an inner strength that she never knew she had. "I'm not glad I had the accident," she told me, "but I'm glad for the confidence I have because of it. I know now that I have the ability to handle really hard and painful challenges."

Some say that courage is being afraid but going on anyhow. Others say that courage is the power to let go of the familiar. To me, courage is both and more. To be resilient we also need what Brené Brown calls "the courage to be vulnerable."[1]

The courage to be vulnerable is the courage to face our doubts, inadequacies, failures, and fears with honesty and acceptance without believing that they define us and without allowing them to defeat us. The courage to be vulnerable gives us the strength to try again. The courage to be vulnerable gives us the confidence to accept the help of another person for the most intimate activities of daily living when we can't do them by ourselves. The courage to be vulnerable makes us willing to try anything that will get us back to living with meaning and purpose in our lives. A young man who survived a spinal cord injury said it this way: ". . . courage can be frustrating and cumbersome, but it is about conquering what is keeping you back . . . and not being embarrassed and hiding behind your disability because all of a sudden you can't go to the washroom, get dressed, or prepare food on your own."[2]

My colleague Virginia didn't have the courage to be vulnerable after she broke her hip (chapter 1). Embarrassed by her need to use a walker, she withdrew from the activities in her senior living community that had been sources of meaning and purpose to her. She said she didn't want to be seen like that. She also dropped out of a study on aging because she didn't think she was a good example of aging well anymore. I think that her need for the walker meant to her that she'd "*failed*" at aging. She felt ashamed and reacted to this feeling by refusing to go out in public where people could see her. But in doing so, she deprived herself of the social interactions and intellectual stimulation that had been sources of energy and enjoyment throughout her life. Because she couldn't continue to be who she'd always been, she gave up trying to live as fully as possible.

I'm certain that the last few years of Virginia's life would have been very different if she'd had the courage to be vulnerable. Then she might have willingly accepted help rather than been embarrassed by needing it. She would have seen her walker as a way to maintain her independence, and she would have continued to participate in the programs and book groups she enjoyed. She might even have been willing to continue as a participant in the study of aging, realizing that her experience was an important contribution to the data. I think her zest for living would have returned, and along with it a renewed inner spirit and a more satisfying quality of life.

Researcher Debra Bournes conducted a study of courage in men who were living with spinal cord injuries. She was interested in how they found ways to move on with their lives amid the challenges of learning to live with the disabilities caused by their paralysis.[3] In examining previous studies of courage, she found that courage had included persistence, determination, tenacity, perseverance, hope and hopefulness, commitment to something valued, self-confidence, fearfulness, and overcoming fear. In her own study, Bournes quoted forty-six-year-old Sam, who said, "Having courage means not letting your inabilities overwhelm what you can do. [Courage is] looking forward to the future instead of living in the past . . . seeing something to do, and aiming for it . . . falling down and getting back up. . . . Regardless of how many times people fall, as long as they are willing to get back up and keep on trying—that's courage . . . and it gives you something to live for."[4]

Perseverance—the drive to keep going toward a goal even when we don't feel like it—joins forces with courage when the need for courage is long-term. Perseverance is the grit that keeps us doing what we need to do to make meaning of our lives in the context of our post-adversity reality. When we keep taking even the smallest of steps toward recovering our sense of well-being after experiencing trauma or adversity, we're engaging our capacity to persevere. All the resilience skills—mindfulness, courage, flexibility, reframing, creativity, realistic optimism, hopefulness, physical activity, spirituality—are enhanced by our ability to persevere—to hang in there, even when the going gets rough and we don't see any immediate gain for doing so.

It's not always easy to persevere. One obstacle that many of us face is a deep-seated sense of failure as a person. I think this was true for Virginia, and it's more common than we might think. Ed Catmull, president of Pixar Animation and Disney Animation, writes about how we're taught from an early age that failure is bad[5]—that it means we didn't try hard enough or that we weren't smart enough or strong enough or good enough to do what we set out to do. We're taught to feel ashamed when we fail. But that's not a helpful way to view failure, he says. It's much better to think of failure as the manifestation of learning and exploration.[6] I think that's the perspective that empowers us to develop the skill of perseverance—viewing all our attempts to deal with the challenges of adversity as manifestations of our desire and willingness to learn and explore.

The things that we try in our efforts to overcome the effects of adversity may not be easy or attractive. Bill, whom you'll meet later, lost both legs to amputation, then taught himself to swim again in a public pool. He had to experiment at every juncture, from crawling all the way from the locker room to the pool's edge to strengthening his body sufficiently to get himself in and out of the pool—all without legs. Bill showed both the courage to be vulnerable and the will to persevere in every aspect of his radical resilience.

Jill Bolte Taylor's recovery after a massive stroke is another example of perseverance and the courage to be vulnerable. She too viewed her work of recovery as the manifestation of learning and exploration rather than as evidence of failure. After the stroke, Taylor had no sense of her body as a physical entity—no sensation of her arms as arms, her legs as legs, or her torso as torso.[7] The sudden hemorrhage in her brain's left hemisphere left her "feeling like a fluid." It also caused changes in her ability to think and to communicate.

Only thirty-seven at the time of the stroke, Taylor began a daily walking routine to help herself become strong again. "I walked with small weights in my hands, swinging my arms here and there, flailing them about like a wild child—but in rhythm," she writes. "I made sure I exercised all of my muscle groups. . . . Lots of people looked at me as if I was odd, but having [also] lost my left hemisphere ego center, I wasn't concerned with their approval or disapproval." Within a year, she was averaging three miles a day, several days a week. Yet even with this focus, and months of regular practice, it took her four years of walking with weights before she could walk with a smooth rhythm again.

Taylor's story of how she overcame the effects of the stroke is evidence of how she engaged the skills that enable us to be radically resilient. She might not, at any given time, have been conscious of drawing on mindfulness, courage, flexibility, creativity, reframing, realistic optimism, hopefulness, and spirituality during the long course of her recovery. But her commitment to persevere toward recovery paid off in much more than the ability to walk in a smooth rhythm again. After a few years, she could also tackle the mental activity of addition. A few months later, she could subtract and multiply as well. And for the first time since the stroke, her mind became capable of doing simple things simultaneously, such as talking on the phone while boiling pasta. Taylor's perseverance in continuing her physical activity undoubtedly boosted her sense of purpose. It boosted her brain's recovery as well.[8] Perseverance is a very powerful resilience skill.

## Some Ways to Practice Courage

**Reflect on difficult experiences in your life.** When did you engage your capacity for courage? Are there times when you didn't engage your courage? Do you see now what you might have done differently to engage your courage in those times?

**Identify something in your life now that you would like to do** that is not dangerous but that you are afraid to do. (For me, it is speaking Spanish with others even though that's the step I need to take to really learn the language.) What do you need to do to have the courage to do what you're afraid to do? Do you need to face a truth about what's holding you back? Self-consciousness, perhaps, or something else? Fear of failure? Shame? Find what you need to help you overcome your reluctance to take action.

**Reflect on having the courage to be vulnerable.** Where do you see opportunities to develop that courage in your life now?

**Practice courage by taking the leap to speak out.** If you are reluctant to speak up in a group to ask questions, offer a different perspective, or raise an issue, you can practice this in private by creating a typical scenario in your mind and thinking of how you might express yourself in ways that will encourage people to listen.

**Practice courage by learning nonviolent communication strategies.** See the end of this book for resources to help you learn how to speak up in charged situations.

**If you're afraid to be involved in any kind of political action,** practice courage by contacting your elected representatives at the local and national levels when you learn of policies that you disagree with and want to protest.

## Some Ways to Practice Perseverance

**Improve your engagement with an ongoing task or activity** that you have been lax about such as exercise or any other activity that benefits from daily practice. When you don't feel like going, remind yourself that you're practicing perseverance—and *go*. If you have difficulty sticking to it, see if another resilience skill such as reframing (chapter 5), flexibility (chapter 4), or learning to overcome an entrenched habit of inactivity (chapter 9) can help you identify and/or overcome the obstacles to your ability to persevere.

**When you become discouraged** because you see someone doing better than you, remember that your process for accomplishing a goal may be different from another's. Keep working toward your goal. Remember *why* you've chosen it and keep going.

**Reframe your experience of failures.** Practice seeing your failures as necessary steps in the process of reaching your goal. They are part of your learning curve. Learn what you can from them and keep going.

**Identify incentives that will keep you going.** Rewards are helpful. Identify a treat that you will enjoy after each treatment. Identify how you will celebrate successes along the way.

**Develop a network of people who are supportive** of your efforts. It helps to have people who listen without judgment, give feedback when asked, and encourage us in our endeavors.

**Don't get dragged down by naysayers.** They're likely to be negative because of their own problems and issues. If you're affected by their attitude, limit the time you spend with them or stop seeing them altogether.

**Start a challenging task and pay attention to the steps you take to accomplish it.** What did you do to help you persevere from the beginning through to the final accomplishment? What were your goals? What obstacles did you face? How did you overcome them? Become familiar with how you approach difficult challenges and the steps you take to overcome them.

Ordinary life provides many opportunities for us to practice courage and perseverance. Whenever we have to make hard decisions that require follow-up, we have an opportunity to consciously practice courage and perseverance. Each time we step outside our comfort zones to accomplish something worthwhile, we're practicing courage in our daily lives.

We build our courage muscles every time we are courageous in facing life's challenges and adversities. We build our perseverance muscles every time we keep moving forward toward a goal even when the process is difficult. These resilience skills sustain us when the going gets tough. They give us the strength to get up in the morning and do the best we can to get through the day. We may not be aware of using them when we're suffering or in pain, but we'll be using them whenever we stay present to our life's journey.

## Summary for Chapter 3: Courage and Perseverance

### What is courage as a radical resilience skill?

- Standing firm in the face of extreme difficulty.
- Facing our doubts, inadequacies, failures, and fears with honesty and acceptance without believing that they define us and without allowing them to defeat us.

### What are some ways to practice courage?

- Identifying something in our life now that we would like to do that is not dangerous but that we are afraid to do, and then doing it. The point is to overcome our fear of doing something we haven't yet had the courage to do.
- Looking for opportunities to sit with our fears and share them with others.
- Learning nonviolent communication strategies so that we can speak with confidence in conversations or meetings where there is disagreement and dissent.

### What is perseverance as a radical resilience skill?

- The continued effort to live a fulfilling life.
- The continued effort to achieve what we desire despite difficulties, failures, or opposition.

What are some ways to practice perseverance?

- Improving our engagement with an ongoing activity that we've been lax about doing regularly.
- Reframing our experience of failures to persevere by seeing them as steps in the process, learning what we can from them, and going on.
- Developing a support network to help us keep on keeping on.
- Maintaining a positive attitude and avoiding people who drag us down.

# 4

# Flexibility

Radical resilience requires flexibility. If we don't have the capacity to both think and act flexibly, we're at a disadvantage when we can no longer do the things that gave our lives meaning and purpose. When we lose the qualities or capacities that have given us our identity—our sense of self—we need the skill of flexibility to adapt to changed circumstances.

A few years ago I went to a museum exhibit of Grandma Moses' paintings and learned about how she began to paint in earnest when she was seventy-eight. Why then? Because the arthritis in her hands became so painful she couldn't continue to make the embroidered pictures and beautiful quilted pieces that she loved to create. She began to express her artistic ideas through painting after her sister suggested that painting might be easier for her. The art world, and the history of American art in particular, is richer because of her flexibility. Anna Mary Robertson Moses didn't stop expressing herself through art when she couldn't do it the way she'd loved to before her arthritis got so bad. She was flexible enough to embark on a new path. That new path led her into a new career—and to considerable fame as well.[1]

Sometimes it's hard to be flexible. When something difficult happens to us and we are hurt or grieving, we may feel lost, overwhelmed, or immobilized. For a while, we may not be able to make decisions or to envision our way forward. What's most important to us then is stability, not flexibility. But after we have recovered from the initial trauma, if we can gradually increase our practice of flexibility, we'll be more resilient in the long run. Studies show that being able to respond flexibly to changing circumstances and being able to control how we express the emotions we're feeling predict better adaptation and adjustment in the daily ebb and flow of living.[2]

This makes me think of Frank, who learned to be flexible the hard way. Frank hated change and had resisted it whenever he could. He wanted as much predictability in his life as possible. For years, he'd opposed any change of plans that his wife Jane suggested, even if it simply meant changing the date of an evening with friends so that she and Frank could attend a concert or a play. Frank said that Jane was always telling him he needed to loosen up. But, he explained, at that time he wasn't interested in loosening up. It wasn't that he objected to going to a concert or a play. He liked both. He simply didn't like to change plans once they were made. He was comfortable only when his life was consistent and orderly.

Then change came. Soon after Frank retired, Jane died. An unexplained infection ravaged her body, and suddenly she was gone. Frank found himself catapulted into a stark new reality. He was devastated by Jane's death and horribly lonely without her.

After a few months, he tried going to his neighborhood senior center. It wasn't long before two women he'd known only slightly began to vie openly for his attention. Each of them brought him cookies, found ways to sit next to him at activities, and kept after him with dinner invitations.

Embarrassed by this attention and confused about how to handle these unwanted advances, Frank quit going. He decided that senior centers were not for him. He tried to fill his time with a variety of volunteer activities, but at the end of the day, the loneliness returned. Nothing Frank did made his loneliness go away.

About a year after Jane's death, Frank woke up at 2 a.m. with severe chest pain. He was able to call 911 and had just managed to get to his front door and unlock it before collapsing on the floor. The next thing he knew he was in the hospital, being readied for coronary bypass surgery.

"That's the experience that turned my life around," Frank said, because participating in the cardio rehab's healthy living program changed his life. He attended a series of classes on emotions, stress management, healthy food, exercise, and lifestyle changes—all things that he could do to improve his energy and strength. After a while, Frank noticed that his perspective on life was different. He began to realize that he'd come through two very tough things: a time of tremendous grief after Jane's death and the trauma of his heart attack. He felt like he'd been in a dark tunnel for a long time, but now he was moving out into the light and ready to start fresh. Frank started remembering how Jane had always encouraged him to loosen up. Now he was ready to try it. In just a few months, he felt confident about making significant changes. He sold their home and bought a condominium near the hospital. He wanted to be able to volunteer there, at the place that had helped him become alive again.

Frank told me that he's learning to practice flexibility. He doesn't do some things in the same way that he's always done them, and a few times a month he'll intentionally try something new. He goes to the senior center in his new neighborhood for a program or two, and he's become more comfortable there than he'd been in the other senior center. The best thing about flexibility, Frank said, is that he's more confident in his ability to handle unexpected occurrences. He still misses Jane. He thinks of her often. But in place of the terrible hurt of grief, there is a memory of shared love. Frank is grateful. He smiles when he says that Jane would be very proud of him.

Frank had to learn about flexibility from scratch. He had to change his attitude toward how to live his life—his mindset—from one that valued consistency and predictability to one that valued flexibility. He had to learn how to be flexible. The cardio rehab program helped him get started. Then he began to practice what he'd learned.

Joan's story about flexibility differs from Frank's. I heard Joan practicing flexibility one day while I was attending a conference with a group of colleagues. As we were returning to the conference center from a field trip, I overheard Joan say to her roommate, "Rather than go out with the group this afternoon, I'm going to stay here and knit. I'm at the point where I need to conserve energy so that I can enjoy tonight's activity."

An active person throughout her life, Joan had found herself increasingly frustrated by limited energy. Medical tests didn't reveal any specific cause for her loss of energy. Joan recognized that the cause was likely to be the stress of her demanding job and the need for her to take a larger role in long-distance caregiving for a parent. She tried to balance those things with her other interests, but she found that after one busy day, she'd be exhausted for several days at a time. Wanting to be resilient rather than upset by her limitations, Joan realized she needed to change her expectations and become more flexible. "I've got to learn to go with the flow," she told her friends.

Her first step was to give herself permission to prioritize activities, to not do so much in a day. She learned to pace herself so she'd have the energy to do the things that were most important to her. She was surprised to find that she could do most of the things she always enjoyed doing, though not necessarily in the same day and not in as short a time as before. After a while she found that she was satisfied doing fewer things each day. Her frustration and fatigue disappeared.

Now Joan is no longer bothered when she experiences limited energy. In fact, she says she's enjoying a more leisurely pace and she sees more interesting things in her environment than she used to. She's much more confident in her ability to handle whatever happens in the future. She even jokes that she sees obstacles that show up in her life as new opportunities to practice flexibility rather than as difficulties she has to overcome.

We get lots of chances to practice flexibility as we go about our ordinary lives. Every time we find our train of thought interrupted or something demands our attention when we're doing something else, or a phone call results in a change of plans, or we get angry about something we can't change, we're given an opportunity to practice flexibility. When we respond to obstacles like these with an intention to practice our flexibility, we're building our capacity to be resilient.

My friend Bonnie has consciously practiced improving her flexibility for several years. Whenever something happens that differs from what she expected, she says—often in a wry tone—"Change is good." Bonnie has discovered that simply saying it out loud, *change is good*, helps her to approach the impending change with a flexible attitude. "I used to get frustrated and out of sorts when I had a day planned and things didn't go according to my plan," she says. "But my little *change is good* mantra makes me laugh. I can feel my frustration giving way. I think it helps me embrace the change so I feel more in control of how I'll respond to it." Saying *change is good* helps her to feel less resentful—sometimes not at all resentful—when she's confronted with a change that is inconvenient or discouraging.

Bonnie has developed an attitude of flexibility by creating her *change is good* mantra. When she's faced with anything that interrupts her day or her plans, the first thing that comes to her mind is *change is good*. This mantra has not only revised her attitude toward change, but it has also set the stage for a flexible action. Saying it to herself creates a positive mental and emotional space that protects her from frustration or resentment and frees her to make a thoughtful decision about how she'll respond. She's proud of herself for creating this way of managing change in her life. She says, "Whatever helps me appreciate what I still have and move forward is good."

Bonnie didn't come to her *change is good* mantra early in life. But she'd been practicing flexibility in the face of life-limiting challenges for years. She'd lived through three very difficult life events: first, the death of a fiancé in the Vietnam War, later the anguish of a mid-life divorce; and years later the sudden death of her second husband after only 16 years of a very happy marriage. Facing life alone once again, yet only in her early sixties, Bonnie realized how much difficult and life-limiting change she'd been through—*and* she recognized that she had come through it well.

Even though each of these difficult experiences took something important away from her, Bonnie is grateful for her life and how things have turned out. And so she can say *change is good* with a sense of rueful confidence. She knows that issues that are difficult now will be resolved at some point. And she feels confident that she'll manage future changes in her life that are hard—because she's done that several times already. She's aware that being flexible helped her to adapt to those changes so she's confident that she'll be able to choose how she'll respond to other changes when they come.

Frank needed to start from the beginning and learn to build flexibility of both attitude and action into his life. This didn't come naturally to him; it was the education he received from the cardio rehab program that taught him what he needed to know about healthier living. The program was a catalyst that helped him see the resilience value of being flexible and to recognize it as the quality that his wife was trying to get him to embrace. Once he learned to embrace flexibility, he could finally move forward in his life.

Joan learned to practice flexibility after finding that she didn't have the energy to do the things she used to do. Instead of giving up, she learned to evaluate competing choices and choose the ones that would best suit her at the time. After a while, Joan found that she could do almost everything she used to do, but not in the same amount of time that she could in the past.

We can see from these three experiences that flexibility has a strong emotional component. Whenever we're faced with a change, we usually have an immediate emotional response such as anger, delight, fear, excitement, anxiety, confusion, embarrassment, among others. Bonnie's mantra *change is good* helps to neutralize her immediate emotional reaction and creates a moment in which she can decide how she wants to respond.

My own mantra, *I'm practicing flexibility*, reminds me to step back from my initial flare of irritation and view what's being required of me with some objectivity. Sometimes though, I simply invoke Bonnie's *change is good*. Like her, I laugh in response to that. Then I'm clear to respond in a more thoughtful way than I might otherwise.

Psychologist Al Siebert identifies flexibility as an absolutely essential ability for resilience.[3] He says that the key to being flexible is to develop what he calls *"oppositional traits,"* such as the ability to be strong *and* gentle, messy *and* neat, humorous *and* serious, logical *and* creative, cooperative *and* rebellious, involved *and* detached, critical *and* non-judgmental, self-critical *and* self-confident. Along with many other seemingly paradoxical pairs of traits, having a range of effective responses is useful when we're confronted by unexpected change or challenge.

Two other aspects of oppositional traits are important components of flexibility as a radical resilience skill. The first is the capacity for *both/and* thinking as opposed to *either/or* thinking. Problems and their solutions are rarely either/or. When we're trying to respond to a difficult challenge, we're often faced with seemingly contradictory ideas on how best to proceed. *Either/or* thinking could lead us to choose the idea we think best. but the best solution might not be any one of them by itself. A *both/and* approach has us consider the merits of each and then, instead of asking "Which of these is the best one?" we'd ask, "How can we combine these ideas to get the best result?" The solution that emerges from our *both/and* thinking may be a combination of some or all the ideas, but it is just as likely to be an entirely new one. Why? Because the *both/and* thinking process engages another resilience skill—creativity—which may reveal possibilities we've not yet explored.[4]

The second oppositional traits component is the capacity for *expressive flexibility*—the ability to both enhance and suppress our emotional expression. Studies show that if we are able to suppress our feelings about something and respond from an opposite emotion if that would be a more appropriate response, we'll be better able to adapt and adjust to life's changes over the long term.[5] For example, we can decide to adjust our expectations of an outcome *from excellent* to *good enough*; we can choose to express how we feel *with emphasis or not*; we can decide to *act bravely when we feel afraid*; or, as we'll see in chapter 5 (Reframing), we can choose to switch mindsets from *judger* to *learner* when we're faced with a change or challenge that we fear or dislike. I like the way Erica Jong describes how expressive flexibility helps her to keep on writing:

> Every poem, every page of fiction I have written, has been written with anxiety, occasionally panic, always uncertainty about its reception. Every life decision I have made—from changing jobs, to changing partners, to changing homes—has been taken with trepidation. I have not ceased being fearful, but I have ceased to let fear control me. I have accepted fear as a part of life, specifically the fear of change, the fear of the unknown, and I have gone ahead despite the pounding in the heart that says: turn back, turn back, you'll die if you venture too far.[6]

Having the inner resources of many opposites greatly increases our capacity to respond appropriately to changes and challenges.

In order to be flexible, we must *want* to be flexible. If we don't want to explore different ideas, different ways to respond to challenges, or see our closely held values from another perspective, then we're not yet in the best state of mind to develop the skill of flexibility. But we can start anyway, simply by being aware of patterns of behavior we could change, and then practicing doing some differently, one small step at a time.

## Some Ways to Practice Flexibility

**Identify something you do regularly. Now, imagine several ways you could do it differently and try them.** Can you use the bus rather than drive? Carpool? I've noticed that using the bus rather than driving enhances my awareness of people and neighborhoods in my city that I don't get if I only drive. For example, I can see people and places as a bus rider that I don't see when driving my car. I become aware of the challenges that people with disabilities or mental illness have when they use public transportation. I like the feeling I get when I use public transportation, a feeling of greater connection to the life of my city.

**Change some of the ways you celebrate holidays or special family events** by serving some different foods, preparing new decorations, or choosing a new way to exchange gifts. As you work with this practice, you may find that there are some you don't want to change and others for which there are many interesting alternatives. You might enjoy thinking about what you like about each alternative, which you prefer, and occasions on which you might use different ones. Your traditional way of celebration may become *just one of the ways* you celebrate in the future.

Use the skill of reframing (chapter 5) to improve your flexibility. Suzanne's childhood illnesses caused her to be very uncomfortable in hospitals. When her husband became ill, she needed to take him to the hospital for treatments and wait there for unpredictable lengths of time. Recognizing her need to become more flexible about spending waiting time in the hospital, she first identified places in which she felt comfortable and safe. Churches were among the places that came to mind, along with many thoughts about what she liked about churches. When she realized that hospitals, like churches, were about healing and helping people, she found a new frame for her attitude about hospitals. In the months that followed, she was at ease with taking her husband to the hospital and waiting for him. She has become more flexible because of her ability to reframe an uncomfortable situation.

Become aware of your use of "should" or "ought" in describing your expectations of yourself or others. Are the expectations you express based on fixed assumptions? In your mind is there only one correct way to be or do that? If so, try to expand your thinking to include other alternatives. Become aware of the things you believe are *"correct" ways* to be or do things. Try to think of alternatives as *other ways* to be or do things rather than as *"wrong" ways*. A friend of mine says that in her money management program, they talk about how it's fine to want whatever you want, *but those desires can't be a requirement for your contentment.*

Do you have fixed ideas about the "right" way that other people should be or act? Or the "right" way your own life has to go for you to be happy? If so, these attitudes and beliefs may describe a limited view that could be severely challenged by a life-changing limitation. For example, some people have the fixed idea that an older person is better off living in their own home regardless of changes in their health and functioning. This idea is often accompanied by the belief that assistance in our own home, if it is needed, is easy to obtain and affordable. Yet neither is necessarily the case. Developing flexibility in this area includes being willing to learn about alternative living communities, visiting them, getting to know people who live in them, identifying some preferences, and envisioning a comfortable transition at the appropriate time if the need occurs. Resources for exploration of senior housing alternatives include local senior centers and the Area Agency on Aging.[7]

**Practice adjusting with flexibility to the realities of your life as they happen.** Like Joan, be realistic about what you can manage, and plan accordingly. Be aware of your priorities so you can evaluate competing choices and choose the one that will be most satisfying to you in the long run. Use your imagination to come up with a mantra that helps you to remember to be flexible. Start with Bonnie's *change is good.* Or with mine, *I'm practicing flexibility.* Create a flexibility mantra that works for you and use it whenever you have to respond to a change you didn't expect. If it helps you to laugh a little and relax, terrific. If it helps you remember that you're practicing flexibility, that's terrific too.

Flexibility is a resilience skill because it helps us respond effectively to change. It keeps us from breaking under stress. As we practice flexibility, we're teaching ourselves how to take change in stride. We begin to see ourselves as successfully adapting to the changes and chances of life. And though we don't look forward to having hard things happen to us, we're developing confidence in our ability to come through life's difficult challenges with our sense of self intact. Our flexibility practice also creates a fertile context for practicing the resilience skill of reframing, which is the subject of the next chapter.

## Summary for Chapter 4: Flexibility

### What is flexibility as a radical resilience skill?

- The ability to adapt to changes as they occur.

### What are some ways to practice flexibility?

- Identifying something we do regularly and imagining several ways we could do it differently.

  - Trying all those ways.
  - After a while, alternating between our two favorite ways.

- Thinking *I'm practicing flexibility* whenever frustrating moments appear in our daily life, then loosening up and responding in a positive way.
- Changing the way we celebrate a holiday or a traditional family event.
- Becoming aware of our use of *should* or *ought* in thinking about or describing our expectations of ourselves or others. Asking whether the expectations we express are based on fixed assumptions or fact? Learning to feel comfortable with other choices that we (or others) make.
- Becoming aware of the things we believe are *"correct" ways* to be or do things. Thinking of alternatives as *other ways* to be or do things rather than as *"wrong" ways*.

# 5

# Reframing

Reframing is to present, look at, or think about something in a new way. Several months after my class on resilience skills, Susan told me how she'd reframed the "horrendously awful" experience of having the sale of her home fall through—for the second time—just before the deal closed. "I was devastated," she said. "It was a time of chaos. We'd already moved out of our large home and rented a smaller one on the other side of town. Our financial situation was horrific. I've always been anxious about money, and now I didn't know what we were going to do."

Discouraged and depressed, Susan wrote her thoughts and feelings in her journal. It was then, she said, that she remembered reframing. She said that when she thought to ask herself how she could reframe her situation, a very clear thought came to her: "Whatever happens, we are not moving back to #1739. We are moving forward. That realization was huge for me. Then, soon after that an image came to me—that we'd been living on an ocean liner and now we're living on a yacht. We'd gotten rid of a lot of stuff, and it felt good to be free of it."

Susan uses her journal as a place for reflection. "Writing in my journal helps me deal with anxiety and chaos. The first two sentences of my journal entry for that time were 'The house

deal fell through on November 30. What will become of us?'
Having the word *reframing* helped a lot. I now have a new perspective on our situation and I'm not so anxious about it."

When we reframe a painting or any other piece of art,
we're looking for a frame that brings out the best in the image.
When we use reframing as a resilience skill, we're exploring
ways to look at our situation from more than one perspective.
It's through this process of exploring different perspectives
that new interpretations of our situation can emerge. Writing
our thoughts in a journal or an ordinary spiral notebook is an
excellent approach to the process of reframing. When we write
what's going on in our heads, the words and feelings that are
internal and amorphous are formed into expressions on a page.
There we can observe them and explore them from varying
points of view. And, as happened for Susan with the ocean
liner and yacht analogy, images can emerge that become the
frame through which we're able to discern a resolution.

But just as choosing a satisfying frame for a piece of art
usually takes several tries, so can reframing a difficult situation.
Not every new perspective will feel better to us than our initial one. But an image, or idea, or some understanding usually
emerges that releases us from the grip of our inner anxiety or
frustration and frees us to imagine a way to move forward.

For example, when the house deal fell through, Susan saw
a picture of financial disaster. But as she was writing about it
in her journal, she remembered that she could reframe this picture. When the thought (frame) came to her that she and her
husband were in fact *not* stuck but in reality were already moving forward, her fear of a disastrous future disappeared. With
fear of disaster gone, she was able to see that they'd found freedom and new life in living on a smaller scale. As an artist, she

understood that the image of "yacht" versus "ocean liner" was a sign that she and her husband were on the right path for them. She then relaxed about the sale of their former home, which sold in due course. Reframing paved the way for Susan to see hope and possibility in a situation that had contained only anxiety and fear.

Susan now frequently uses reframing to get a fresh perspective on troubling situations. When her husband suddenly lost consciousness one day, she was terrified. In a haze of fear and anxiety, she managed to call 911. The ambulance came right away. As she watched the ambulance drive away with her husband inside, she felt an overwhelming surge of a long-ago fear of being alone. Not feeling up to driving, she called a friend to take her to the hospital. For the next couple of days, Susan lived in a state of shock, waiting anxiously for updates from the doctors. She was inwardly shaking until she knew her husband would be all right.

In telling me about her experience a few weeks later, Susan thanked me for teaching her about reframing. "I found that this time I couldn't do it right away," she said. "I tried to reframe while I was waiting in the hospital for the updates and I just couldn't do it then. It took a couple of days before I was able to see the situation in a different frame." She told me that as she was thinking about everything that had happened, she reframed by asking herself what had worked amid all that confusion and stress.

"I realized that when I had called for help, help had come quickly," she said. "The ambulance had come right away. Friends came to drive me and be with me for hours. Both of our sons [who live elsewhere] were at their homes when I called. I saw that I hadn't been alone for very long. And suddenly I felt a release of internal chaos." Susan paused. Then she said, "Reframing made me realize that my network of family and friends is secure. I was able to see that whatever happened, I would not be alone."

Robert Coles has written about how the stories in literature can help us reframe our own stories.[1] Coles is a psychiatrist whose early work was in a hospital. He writes about Phil, a fifteen-year-old who had lost the use of both legs after contracting polio. Phil was alone in the world except for a grandmother and a couple of faraway uncles. He had been in the hospital about a week when he realized that he wasn't just sick. He was really paralyzed, and it might be for a lifetime.

The realization that his paralysis had changed his life forever threw him into a deep depression. "He became morose," writes Coles. "All he could think of was 'the black space' of his future life." A teacher from Phil's school came to the hospital to visit him from time to time. Coles described the teacher as a gentle, quiet man. He was "real," neither talkative nor cheery. He spent much of his time with Phil sitting in silence or listening. One day he quietly left a book on Phil's bedside table. It was Mark Twain's *The Adventures of Huckleberry Finn*.

Phil wondered why the teacher had brought it—he'd already read the book in class the previous year with no particular interest. But he picked it up one day, and this time he couldn't put it down. He told Coles, "I read, and when I was done with the story, I felt different. I can't tell you, I can't explain what happened; but I know that my mind changed after I read *Huckleberry Finn*. . . . I forgot about myself—no, I didn't actually. I joined up with Huck and Jim; we became a trio . . . I talked with those guys, and they straightened me out!"[2]

Later, Phil became captivated by the story of Holden Caulfield in Salinger's *The Catcher in the Rye*. As he read and reread Holden's story, he began to glimpse a sense of purpose for his own life. Although he read other stories, he returned often to Huck and Holden. These stories stirred Phil, writes Coles. They brought him to reflection. Phil didn't like being paralyzed, but he did like having an emerging sense of vision for his life.

"I've seen a lot, lying here," Phil told Coles. "I think I know more about people, including me, myself—all because I got sick and can't walk. It's hard to figure out, how polio can be a good thing. It's not, but I like those books, and I keep reading them, parts of them, over and over."[3]

Coles saw that reading those stories enabled Phil to reframe the picture of his future. They gave him hope. Until he had read and reread them, Phil had seen no use for any further schooling. But now he began to consider what kind of education he wanted, given his special difficulties. His picture of his future as unending black space was replaced by a future that held possibility and meaning.

## When Reframing, Pay Attention to Mindset

I've learned from the work of Marilee Adams the importance of paying attention to our mindset when we're trying to reframe a situation. Adams has developed a process that she calls "Question Thinking."[4] It's a way of using questions to direct our thinking when we're faced with a problem, a change, or a challenge and we're stuck in negative thoughts and emotions about it. The Question Thinking process begins with identifying our mindset.

Adams identifies the mindsets that we use when dealing with problems, changes, and challenges as the "judger" mindset and the "learner" mindset. The *judger* mindset is not about judgment; it's about being judgmental. *The judger* mindset is reactionary; it makes us want to defend ourselves and blame others. We also make judgmental statements and ask closed-ended questions that cut off the possibility for raising other perspectives on the issue. Some examples of *judger*-mindset thinking are "Whose fault is it?" "What's wrong with them?" "How could you do such a thing?" "That's ridiculous."

*The judger* mindset thinking can also be self-directed, exemplified in thoughts like "What's wrong with me?" "Why am I such a failure?" and "I'm so stupid!" This outlook drains our energy and closes off our capacity for creative thinking.

The *learner* mindset is an inquiry mindset that allows us to be open to learning more about ourselves and to inviting other people's perspectives on the situation. Some examples of *learner* mindset thinking are "What assumptions am I making?" "What are my choices?" "What is the other person feeling, needing, or wanting?" "What can I learn from this?" "What other ways can I look at this?" *This way of thinking* opens us to creative thinking and thus leads to successful reframing.

Question Thinking is a process that expands the concept of reframing and makes it a very powerful resilience skill. We can see this at work in the following story.

Margaret, a fiercely independent woman in her early sixties, knew that her diagnosis of macular degeneration meant that at some point she'd no longer be able to drive her car. Being able to drive was very important to Margaret—driving gave her freedom and independence. She could go wherever and whenever she wanted to. But since she lived in a suburban community with no public transportation, she realized that ultimately she'd either have to find alternative transportation or move.

Margaret could still see pretty well, so she thought that she'd probably have a couple of years to decide what to do. So she was shocked to hear her doctor tell her just a few months later that it was definitely time for her to stop driving. To Margaret, this sudden and unexpected news meant that she would soon become blind. Depressed and frightened by this prospect, she fell into a *judger* mindset. She wondered what she had done wrong to have this happen. She beat herself up with thoughts about how she "should have" taken better care of her eyes, about how she "should have" paid more attention to nutrition. These thoughts hounded her. "I should have looked into assisted living when I got the diagnosis," she lamented. She'd landed into what Adams calls *"the judger pit,"* wondering why she was such a failure.

After a week or so, Margaret's sense of self as a competent person bubbled up in her. She reminded herself that she'd solved difficult challenges in the past. She remembered that she had a large group of friends who said they would help if she needed it. Her thought process had switched out of *judger* mindset and moved her into *learner* mindset. Now she asked herself, "What are the facts? What assumptions am I making? What can I learn? What do I want? What are my choices? What's best to do now?" She consulted with her doctor and discovered that with ongoing treatment, her eyesight would likely be stable for some time. Further deterioration might occur, but it might not. Only time would tell.

With the knowledge that she would be able to see well enough to function in many ways other than for driving, Margaret decided to explore possibilities for services that would meet her current needs. She would ask friends for assistance only if other options were not available. She arranged with her senior center for transportation services and some household help. She contracted with an organization that purchased and delivered groceries, and she arranged for the household helper to come on the same day the groceries arrived. And with the knowledge that her eyesight might deteriorate further down the road, Margaret applied for an assistance dog and decided to learn Braille. She also began to research assisted living communities that would meet her needs if she should need to move to one in the future.

For Margaret, the shift from *a judger* mindset to *a learner* mindset made an immense difference in how she felt about herself. It gave her the energy and optimism to look for solutions outside of her friendship network, thus maintaining her independence. Working through her plans from the perspective of a learner helped her to see how she could include her friends by asking them to do the things that she needed that weren't available otherwise.

Like Margaret, most of us are in *a judger* mindset when we are first confronted with a challenge, a problem, a broken relationship, or a life-changing adversity. Feelings rise up in us and demand our attention. We have to acknowledge them before we can move beyond them. We need to be aware of our mindset and recognize if we are still reacting to what has happened and are heading down the *judger* path. If we are, do we want to be there? Or are we ready to switch to a *learner* mindset and consider other perspectives that will move us forward in positive ways?

When I was hospitalized many years ago, some of my family and close friends were busy with responsibilities that kept them from being as supportive of me as I would have liked. Although other friends and acquaintances came to visit, ran errands, sent cards and flowers, and were very present to me for the whole time I was in the hospital, I felt a lot of resentment toward those few who, in my view, should have been there more for me.

Months later, when I had recovered and was reflecting on the whole experience, I realized that all my needs had been met during that time in the hospital—they just hadn't been met by some of the people I had expected would meet them. I also realized that those people had done as much as they could under the circumstances of their own lives. Suddenly I felt as if a light had turned on inside me. All the bitterness and negativity that my resentment had bred inside me was gone.

Though I didn't know then about reframing, or about *judger* and *learner* attitudes, I knew that something had happened to help me see my experience from an entirely different point of view. Somehow, I had let go of my *judger* mindset and reflected on my experience as a *learner*. I saw that my needs had been met in abundance—that I'd received everything that I'd needed and much more. I felt that I'd been taken care of, supported, and loved by a large network of people, including by those whom I had felt "should have" done more. I was no longer stuck in resentment. Instead, I experienced an overwhelming sense of humility and appreciation that more than enough people had reached out to meet my needs and be there for me in that very difficult time.

Now that I know about Question Thinking and about the *judger/learner* mindsets, I've found them to be helpful for honest reflection, self-awareness, and positive communication. They are powerful tools that support all the resilience skills.

I'm glad to know about the *judger* mindset because it helps me to recognize and name the times that I hold a judgmental attitude about someone, which reminds me to move past them. But sometimes, recognizing that I'm in *judger mode* leads me to dig deeper into my feelings to see *why* I'm there, and ask myself *what* I need to do to move into *a learner mentality*. Adams' insights not only give us a specific method for honest reflection, self-awareness, and positive communication; they're also designed to guide us when we face the challenging realities of change, conflict, or adversity.

The purpose of reframing is not to ignore reality or engage in unrealistic fantasy. Reframing means that we engage our imaginations in generating a number of different ways we might interpret or understand our situation or experience. Some of the possibilities we imagine may seem so preposterous they make us laugh. But that's good. Laughter relaxes us and eases tension.

The right frame will be the one that changes the way we see our situation so that we feel "unstuck" and can move forward with next steps. If we still feel stuck after a session of reframing, we give ourselves a break and try again later. The process itself will most likely have opened our minds, imaginations, and hearts to new perspectives on the challenges that we face.

## Some Ways to Practice Reframing

When we experience frustration, ask ourselves: "How can I reframe this?" or "What's another way I can look at this?" Just asking these questions sets our mental stage for thinking about our situation differently. Asking the question, **"What can**

I learn from this?" engages our brain in a thinking response and helps to neutralize the agitation we feel when we're frustrated.

Examine our assumptions. These are the beliefs about what is right or true that we take for granted. They're beliefs that we've been taught by our parents or our culture, or that we have learned from our own experience, but we've never questioned their truth. When we're upset about something, we first have to examine our assumptions. **What did we assume would happen instead of what did happen? Why? Do we understand all the facts? If yes, do the facts support our assumptions?**

The assumptions on which we base our emotions and our thinking often turn out to be wrong. That happened for Margaret, who assumed that since her vision had declined to the point that she couldn't drive, she'd soon be blind. When she discovered that her assumption was not correct, that her vision would not necessarily continue to rapidly decline, Margaret could reframe her situation and see how to develop a plan that would sustain her independence.

Use Question Thinking to get unstuck from unhelpful attitudes and behaviors. It's important to practice identifying our mindset when we're trying to reframe. Ask "Am I in *a judger or a learner* mindset?" It may take a few tries to recognize our *judger* mindset and to be willing to switch to that of a *learner*, but we'll want to do so as soon as we can. Once we've switched, we're ready to ask the questions that will put us on the path toward resolution.

Adams refers to this process of asking questions as the "path" we take toward an outcome. Questions that take us down the *judger* path (to the *judger pit*) are questions like "What went wrong? "Who's to blame?" and "How could you do that?"

When we go down *judger* path, we not only get increasingly angry and frustrated, we cause anyone else involved in the issue to become tense and defensive.

*Learner* path questions are ones such as "What assumptions am I making? "What are the facts?" "Have I asked others what they are thinking or feeling about the issue?" "How else can I think about this?" take us in a positive direction. This type of question is respectful of everyone involved, including ourselves, creating an emotionally healthy context for the reframing process.

**Reject unnecessary limitations.** I learned this valuable advice many years ago from Healthwise, Inc.[5] A careful examination of our assumptions may reveal that we've accepted limitations about our situation because we think that nothing can be done to change or overcome them. For example, when Margaret realized that there were ways that she could do many of the things she enjoyed even after she could no longer see, she understood that she'd been holding on to an unnecessary limitation—that blindness would stop her from doing the things that were part of her identity. Letting go of this unnecessary limitation freed Margaret to plan and arrange for the services and training she would need to live independently.

Have you ever been told "no, that's not possible" by a customer service person and accepted that as truth? That nothing further could be done? I used to, until a friend who had worked in several travel agencies gave me this tip: If we don't get the response we want, just say thank you, and end the call. Then, call back. If we're dealing with a large company, we're very likely to get a different person. Then, supported by our *learner* mindset, we politely tell the new person what we want and that we hope they'll be able to help us. Very often, that person will find that what we request is indeed possible, and they'll help us get it. Sometimes it takes a few tries, but often it only takes a second call. Every once in a while we find through our process of inquiry that the limitation is real. Then we know we're dealing with a fact rather than an assumption, and we can choose another reframing strategy to find a resolution.

**Read good fiction and nonfiction—they're excellent resources for reframing.** When we connect with the characters in literature, there's often something in their story that can give us insight and perspective into our own life. Is a particular character facing challenges similar to ours? How does this character respond to challenges? What does this character fear? What does the character do? How does what the character does turn out for them?

We can learn something about ourselves when we pay attention to the characters in literature that we connect with. We can often see something about a character's choices that give us insight into our own. That insight may even cause us to change what we do. Through literature we also can see aspects of our own situation that we didn't see before. Nonfiction books that provide stories of other peoples' experience with situations similar to ours can also show us ways to reframe our own. Sometimes, we see the possibility of resolution that we couldn't even imagine before we read a particular book or story.

Many of my friends enjoy discussing books—both fiction and nonfiction—in a group with others they trust. They find that that their discussion of a book complements their individual reading of it. Often, those discussions give rise to new or broader perspectives on the readers' lives as well as on the lives of the characters they read about.

**Write down your thoughts, concerns, fears, hopes, dreams.** Writing (longhand) in a notebook or journal helps get our thoughts out of our heads and onto a piece of paper where we can see them. Often, that's enough to give us a different perspective on whatever we want to reframe. When I was working in a particularly challenging job, I kept a spiral notebook in my car. At the end of a complicated day, I'd stop at the library that was on my route between work and home. I'd take my notebook out of the pocket of the back seat, find a spot at a table in the library, and write whatever came into my head about the day.

I usually wrote two to three pages nonstop, ending with some concrete tasks I would do the next day. The action of stopping and writing for twenty minutes or so helped me to reframe the day from being one of multiple problems that needed solving to one that now had focus and perspective. Just the action of writing about the day moved my tangled thoughts and feelings from inside—where they just kept going around mostly in my head (though often I felt them in my gut too)—to outside, where they were on paper. Very soon after writing I felt their power over me diminish. As I got back into the car to drive home, I felt centered, ready to enjoy the evening at home.

A friend tells me that if she's having a problem with someone, she'll often write in her journal not only the problem (and solution) from her perspective, but also the problem (and a possible solution) from the other person's perspective. She says that putting the other person's thoughts into her own words helps her to see her own position in a different light. The result? After doing this particular reframing practice, she can usually see a resolution that satisfies both parties. I see this as her *learner* mindset in action, doing its work of opening us to inquiry and to the process of discovery about the other person's needs and point of view. That *learner* work is what creates the context for discerning a resolution that satisfies both parties.

Reframing is a powerful resilience skill. Using one or more of these reframing strategies will help us to clarify our challenges and identify ways to move toward resolution.

The following chapter introduces another powerful resilience skill—one we're born with but have usually lost touch with by the time we're teenagers. It's creativity—and we'll learn how to reclaim it—or develop it further—as a vital resource for radical resilience.

## Summary for Chapter 5: Reframing

### What is reframing as a radical resilience skill?

- Exploring different perspectives on a concern or situation to get unstuck from a perspective that is not helpful.
- Thinking about a concern or situation in new ways.

### What are some ways to practice reframing?

- Being in a *learner* mindset when we reframe.
- Asking "How can I reframe this?" or "What's another way I can look at this?" whenever we feel frustrated, confused, angry or upset about something.

- ○ Sometimes "What can I learn from this?" fits the situation better.

- ○ All three questions can free us from feeling that our initial response to the situation is the only interpretation possible.

- Examining our assumptions when something happens that's different from what we expected. What did we assume would happen? What do the facts support?

# 6

# Creativity

reativity is a crucial skill for radical resilience because it fuels our ability to explore ideas, see new possibilities, and solve problems. We're all born with a natural drive toward creativity, yet by the time we're adults, many of us believe that we're not at all creative. Somehow our instinct toward creative exploration and expression gets curbed during our growing-up years. Maybe it's because teachers and parents hurt or embarrass us with criticism. Maybe we're teased about our creative efforts. Maybe our joy in creating is shut off by an adult who insists on showing us how to "do it right."

I remember the November morning our four-year-old son refused to get ready to go to preschool. "I don't want to go," he insisted. This was new behavior, and it concerned me. Why did he suddenly not want to go to the school he had loved for almost three months?

I called the teacher to let her know he wouldn't be there and made an appointment to meet with her in her classroom after school. The classroom was decorated with bright, cheerful Thanksgiving-themed images. On one wall were posters of pilgrims, pumpkins, and cornstalks. On the opposite wall, prominently displayed, were the children's paintings of turkeys. I did a double-take when I looked at this display—it startled me. Everything about these turkeys matched: the size, the colors, the placement on the paper, the brush strokes. Only the names on the paintings differed. Fourteen different four-year-olds had painted fourteen identical turkeys.

"Tell me a little about these turkeys," I said to the Montessori-trained teacher. "They look all the same to me."

"Yes!" she exclaimed, appearing very pleased that I had noticed. "I stand behind the children and guide their hand while they paint," she said. "That way the turkeys all come out looking very nice."

I was horrified. I knew then exactly why my son didn't want to go back to this school. He must have felt imprisoned in that painting session. Although he was an attentive kid who didn't mind following directions, he was used to having much more freedom than this when doing creative activities. I think he felt shut down that day. Of course he didn't want to go back. And he didn't have to. We found a different preschool for him—one in which the teachers were committed to encouraging creative expression and exploration in each of their young students.

When we're stifled in our creative endeavors or when our creative expression is criticized by someone else—teacher, parent, sibling, friend, it doesn't matter who—we quickly develop our own inner critic. Our inner critic's job is to evaluate our creative work before anyone else has a chance. Our inner critic is quick to point out flaws in our artwork, mistakes in our music playing, clumsiness in our expressive movement, or any negative aspect of whatever creative activity we're engaged in. Our inner critic also likes to predict the future, telling us things like *"You'll never be good at this."* So it's not surprising that over time many of us come to assume that we're not creative. But that's an assumption, not a fact. And assumptions always need to be examined to see if they are really true or not. For the truth is that our natural creativity is still inside us.

## Creativity and Resilience

We've probably drawn on our natural creativity many times in our lives without realizing it. That's because creativity is a multi-faceted skill that encompasses all the ways we use our imagination to see new ways to solve problems, do tasks, think new thoughts, understand new meanings, find a new use for something, or make something new. Creativity is much more than artistic ability—it is also the ability to think of more than one possibility in response to a given idea, situation, or challenge. Creativity can be expressed through the sciences and technology as well as through the arts. In fact, creativity can be expressed in multiple ways in our daily lives.

We expressed our creativity when we were children learning to live in a new, unfamiliar, exciting, and sometimes threatening world. We'd make up songs and stories, thrill to the sensation of making mud pies and later of working with clay. We'd build structures with blocks or Lego and then knock them down so we could put those pieces together a different way. We'd dress up in costumes, dance to music, create tunes on a keyboard, and make colorful pictures of the things in our world that we loved. We expressed joy and sadness, boldness and inquisitiveness, freedom, pleasure, and many other aspects of our inner thoughts and feelings through our creative activity. Expressing ourselves through our creativity helped us—and continues to help us—become who we are.

There's an element of play in creativity that loosens us up and energizes us. Being relaxed from play helps us be attuned to new ideas, new images, new directions, and a new sense of self. Play is called *recreation* for a reason: it re-creates us. That spark of re-creation ignites our capacity for resilience and provides the energy to go forward.

"Creativity," writes Gene Cohen, ". . . is a process or an outlook, not a product. It is a distinctly human quality that exists independent of age and time, reflecting a deeper dimension of energy capable of transforming our lives at any age."[1]

Creativity includes the ability to imagine connections between disparate objects. This kind of creativity often comes as we're *"playing around"* with ideas or observations and a creative connection jumps out at us. That's how Velcro was invented. A thistle got stuck in a hiker's sock. The hiker—George de Mestral—wondered how something could penetrate both his sock and his dog's fur so easily—yet be so difficult to remove. Would this be useful for something? Though it took him a decade to succeed, he kept using his creative imagination to invent one of the most useful tools of the twentieth century.[2]

Creative expression through play, the arts, scientific discovery, technology, innovation, and invention enhances our resilience because it enables us to express our inexpressible inner self in a way that we can see as well as integrate what we couldn't express in thought or word. We don't have to be "an artist" to benefit from this aspect of creativity. We can simply play around with color, or movement, or sound, or words or any other medium that captures our imagination and engages us in doing something with it. "Wherever the soul is in need," writes Shaun McNiff, "art presents itself as a resourceful helper."[3]

## Creativity as Self-Expression through Play and the Arts

Soon after her fiftieth birthday, Kathe LeBeau found the play that nourished her soul—she discovered the performing art of clowning. Scheduled for a surgery workup for gallbladder issues, LeBeau was told that her kidneys were only functioning at 35 percent of their ability. At first she couldn't believe it. "I can't possibly be sick, I feel fine!" she thought. "It's a silent disease—it sneaks up on you. You just feel more and more tired. . . . I had to leave the job that I loved because of the fatigue that comes with kidney disease. I had always been very active and now I was looking at four walls, sitting in a chair at home. I could walk to the mailbox and back. I had no idea if this is what I was going to be looking at for the rest of my life."[4]

A year of home hemodialysis treatment pulled LeBeau back into the land of the living. She started working and traveling again. "I was searching for things that would put joy back into my life." A flier in the mail one day advertised a twelve-week clowning class at a local community college. She signed up and loved it. She wanted to be a sweet, jolly, silly clown that made kids feel comfortable. But it took a while for LeBeau to get comfortable. "It takes a little while to get your head around the idea of being a clown. It's about working on letting go of any inhibitions and not being afraid of being silly."

LeBeau made clowning a regular part of her life. She fit it in with the limitations of her disease, which included fatigue from regular dialysis treatments. She named her clown Kismet, who performed a couple of times a month for pediatric kidney patients. Clowning has been fun, she said, and has saved her from isolation and despair.

What would LeBeau say to people who want to follow their dreams but are afraid to? "Don't let one day get too far away from you," she said passionately. "That's the other piece of why I started clowning . . . I really had no idea how much life I was looking at. We all take for granted the fact that we have endless amounts of days. Make sure that you're doing the things that are important, that you've always wanted to do. That sort of crystallized it for me. You just don't waste time."[5]

Jeremy Nobel, a critical care physician and faculty member of the Harvard School of Public Health, is the founder and president of the Foundation for Art and Healing.[6] He summarizes the major benefits of creative expression through the arts in this way:

> Art allows you to do three things, and this is where the healing comes from. Art puts you in the moment, puts you in touch with yourself and allows you to bring forth something that did not exist before. And those three things taken together are incredibly powerful in terms of adjusting your understanding of yourself, your relationship to yourself, your relationship to the world and your sense about possibilities for the future.[7]

The experiences of Julia and Grace, two women who've lived for many years with myalgic encephalomyelitis (ME), support Nobel's findings.[8] ME is a progressively debilitating, painful disease that affects the whole body.[9] It is caused by a viral infection that attacks the brain and central nervous system.

After five years of feeling that her life had lost its meaning to the restriction and unpredictable disorder of this disease, Julia recognized that she wasn't going to improve much more. She'd reached a plateau.

At this critical point, Julia decided to live with this reality and began to search for a life-affirming activity that she could do within the restrictions of her health. She found that she could design and make a variety of small textile arts and crafts items for charity if she selected items that were light enough to handle with minimal fatigue. Working with color and creating new designs became sources of enjoyment and satisfaction for her. "Art-making has made a difference to my life. . . . It was as though . . . the door was ajar and suddenly someone flung it open and said 'this is it' . . . that's the way forward. . . . I've got something else to turn to rather than just looking at the things that I can't do."

Another benefit for Julia was the joy she experienced in being able to participate in charitable activity, something she had enjoyed before she got sick. The idea that she could make lovely things and give them to charity boosted her sense of self and restored continuity to her life.

Watercolor painting became the way that helped Grace live positively within the confines of ME. Grace described her experience of painting like this:

> Somehow it seems to make it authentic and valid, you know . . . that the feelings that I had were valid and they were authentic, because I'd made them real and I'd put them on paper. . . . I didn't realize when I was starting to paint just how important an outlet it was going to be to me. But when did I start? . . . probably about twelve years now

and yes, I don't quite know what I would have done without it. . . . I've realized for a long time now that I need to spend as much of my time as I possibly can doing the most positive things that I can, and maximizing my quality of life and if anything's going to get me better, in the absence of somebody discovering a miracle, that is going to be the way to do it. So, it isn't just the art, it's everything.

Music—either listening to it or making it—also has the power to transform how we feel about ourselves and our life. I remember walking past my seminary chapel when I was studying for my degree in religious education many years ago. I was feeling fragmented, unsure if I wanted to keep going to the end of the term, when the sounds of a Bach fugue stopped me. I stood spellbound as an organ student practiced the piece, sometimes playing and replaying certain phrases and then moving on to play longer sections. As the student practiced, I became aware of how the shifting harmonies and multiple musical lines of the fugue reflected the interactive play of conflict and resolution in my life. In just a few moments, my sense of being overwhelmed by the demands of my life transformed into a sense that the music, moving rapidly forward, was mirroring the internal conflict that I was feeling. "This is how life goes too," I thought. Conflict, tension, resolution—then more tension, conflict, and resolution. But this process, expressed through music, is *beautiful.* My tensions subsided as I stood at the chapel window and listened. I began to feel calm inside. When the piece came to its end, I felt a surge of energy, of inspiration. I went on my way, a changed person.

Studies show that listening to music that we like can significantly decrease pain, depression, anxiety, and even disability.[10]

Somehow, the creative expression that lies within the music affects our brains in ways that positively influence our physical, mental, and emotional systems. All we have to do is really listen.

Oliver Sacks in his book *Musicophilia* cites some examples of how listening to music and/or making music has helped people walk again, talk again, or control the unpredictable symptoms of Tourette's Syndrome.[11] He cites the memoir of Nick, a young English musician:

> When I played, my tics almost seemed to disappear. It was like a miracle. I would tic, gyrate, and verbally explode all day at school, get home exhausted from it all and run to the piano and play for as long as I could, not only because I loved the sounds I was making, but primarily because when I played I didn't tic. I got time off from the ticcy normality that had become me.[12]

Tobias Picker, a distinguished composer who also has Tourette's, finds that when he is composing or playing the piano, his tics also disappear.[13]

## Creativity as Making Connections between Disparate Things

Author, educator, and creativity expert Ken Robinson describes creativity as making fresh connections so that we see things in new ways and from different perspectives.[14] We see this aspect of creativity in the following story of Janet, eighty-two, who'd experienced a debilitating stroke, and her adult son Roger.[15]

Several months after the stroke, Janet was discharged from physical therapy even though her left arm was still paralyzed and she couldn't use it. "You've improved as much as possible," the therapist told her. Medicare wouldn't cover the cost of any more sessions.

Janet was devastated. She'd worked hard at the exercises that the therapist had given her. She wanted to be able to crochet again, to make the beautiful vests, shawls, and bed coverings that she'd loved to create and give to friends and family. Crocheting also kept her busy and gave her something to do as she listened to music or books on tape. Now, her permanent left-side paralysis meant that she would never be able to crochet again.

Roger was concerned about his mom. He knew that the discharge from physical therapy was a great blow to her. It took away her hope that one day she would finally be able to crochet again. Janet became increasingly depressed despite her continued efforts to remain positive. Roger didn't know how to help her.

One day, as he was using his workbench, Roger looked at the vice affixed at the end. Suddenly, he saw it from a new perspective. He started to wonder if the vice could hold a crochet hook in such a way that his mother could work the crochet thread around it with her good hand.

He began to experiment with various ways to firmly attach the vice to a table so that the jaws of the vice would be sideways, thus able to hold a crochet hook horizontally. He imagined the vice and crochet hook combination as a stable substitute for his mother's paralyzed left arm and hand. Optimistic that he'd hit on something that would work, he kept experimenting until he found a way to replicate his vision on his dining room table. Then Roger called his mother and told her he had a surprise for her.

Janet could not believe her eyes as she watched Roger install his invention on her dining room table. Overjoyed that she had not given away all her crochet materials, she sat down to experiment with using her right hand to manipulate the thread around the stationery crochet hook. It took only a few minutes for her to feel comfortable with this new setup. Before long she was able to crochet to her heart's content. Janet was thrilled. No longer depressed by the loss of self-expression, Janet regained her emotional energy and her enjoyment of life. She began to entertain visitors in her home. The despondency that had plagued her for many months disappeared.

Creativity as making connections between disparate things has led to innovations in many disciplines. Peter Pronovost's insight regarding the role of the airline pilot's mandatory checklist is an example.[16] Pronovost, an anesthesiologist at Johns Hopkins Hospital in Baltimore, connected what he knew about the airline pilot's checklist with a critical need to decrease the rate of infections that were occurring in hospital patients who receive central line catheters. Pronovost developed and tested a checklist for pre-surgery procedures that resulted in an immediate reduction in the incidence of central line infections at Johns Hopkins. Sometime later, the state of Michigan initiated a pilot project to use Pronovost's checklist in Michigan hospitals. The incidence of central line infections from catheters in those hospitals also declined dramatically. Now used in hospitals across the United States, the Pronovost checklist is credited with saving many thousands of lives every year.[17]

I too experienced a sense of accomplishment from making a connection between disparate objects when I discovered how to turn a Lucite and metal over-the-door coat hook into a Kindle holder for a treadmill. I'd wanted to solve the problem of boredom on the treadmill during my cardio rehab sessions. I'd seen a friend in the program use his much smaller Sony e-reader on the treadmill and I asked him about it. He explained how he'd adapted two plastic boxes that electricians use and then added some Velcro to create the holder for his Sony. I was impressed by my friend's creativity but I wanted something less complicated. So I put the problem to rest. However, as often happens with creativity, my mind kept working on it, surfing constantly underneath my conscious awareness for something that might solve the problem.

A few weeks later I was in a TAP Plastics store, looking for plastic photograph frames. A display of over-the-door coat hooks suddenly caught my eye. Being a multitasker, I stopped to examine the hooks because I needed something like that for my office door. The coat hooks were shaped like the letter *J*. They were made of Lucite, with an adjustable metal part on the top to fit over a door. The *J* was about one inch wide and seven inches high. I picked one up, held it, and studied it in relation to using it on my office door to hold coats. Suddenly, a picture of the cardio rehab treadmill flashed in my mind. As I began to envision how this coat hook might fit on the treadmill, I was surprised to hear myself burst out, loud enough that others turned to hear, "I wonder if *this* would work."

I bought the coat hook and could hardly wait to get back to the cardio rehab treadmill. I tried it as I had envisioned, with the Lucite *J* upside down to hook over the treadmill's display panel. The adjustable metal *L* then faced up to hold the Kindle. Although this worked fine, I could see right away that it might be better if I turned it around so that the metal part was adjusted to fit over the top of the display pane. Yes—it was just right.

Emboldened by my success, I bought a second hook so that together they could accommodate my larger, heavier iPad. That was also a success. I was thrilled. Lightweight, portable, and adjustable, these coat hooks made it possible for me to read while working out on the treadmill in the cardio rehab gym.

The best bonus, though, came from the experience itself. I found that the process of getting an unexpected idea—then trying it, adapting it, and having it work—released a flow of life-affirming energy in me that has continued to nourish my spirit ever since. I experienced for myself the evidence that our minds work on things we're trying to understand—or problems we're trying to solve—even when we're not consciously aware of thinking about them. It also showed me the truth of Gene Cohen's observation: creativity is an ongoing process that engages our senses, our imaginations, our sense of play, our unconscious material, and our conscious thought, *to enrich our lives from start to finish.*

Yet I suspect that we tend to shy away from engaging in creativity because we're afraid of failure. We don't want our creative efforts to result in something that doesn't work, doesn't look right, tastes terrible, or results in any unsuccessful outcome. That would simply be too embarrassing. But we can't expect to create—or even do—something new without failing. So rather than be embarrassed or discouraged by our failures, we can learn what we can from them and keep on going.

Creativity, writes Ken Robinson, is *applied imagination.* It transforms the present in some way.[18] Most if not all the stories of radical resilience in this book are of people who have applied their imaginations to come through an adverse happening that has changed their life. They've overcome their fear of failure and they go forward even through moments of embarrassment. Jill Taylor, in chapter 3, went for regular walks in her neighborhood even though her walking was haphazard and she looked awkward. Bill, in chapter 8, retaught himself how to swim in a public pool after he'd lost both legs to amputation. Grace and Julia, in this chapter, applied their imaginations toward discovering what they *could* do to live meaningful lives within the confines of a debilitating illness.

The resilience skills work separately and together to move us toward discovering purpose in our lives and restoring our sense of self when we can't do what we've always done to be ourselves. There's an element of creativity in each of the resilience skills. Yet creativity in its own right is a powerful tool for self-expression. It takes us out of ourselves into a realm of exploration and discovery, be it in our imaginations or expressed in numerous other ways.

## Some Ways to Practice Creativity

If you think you're not creative, you may want to start with this. Think about your own early school years. Were you taught things at a young age that stifled your creativity? Were you taught that certain items are to be used only for certain things? That poems are supposed to rhyme? That flowers are red but not green, that leaves are green but not purple, that sky is always blue? Were you taught that making up silly connections between words or objects is just that, silly? That unless something has a purpose or is useful, it isn't worth doing, isn't worth making?

You might find it helpful to take a few minutes to write down some of the comments, instructions, or feedback you received as a child or youth when you were engaged in creative, imaginative expression. Include comments that were encouraging as well as those that were discouragingly critical. Remember that creativity is expressed in many ways including, but not limited to, artistic expression. What was the setting for your creativity? Was it practicing an instrument and trying out new sounds with it? Was it trying a science experiment? Was it building a structure with blocks or reading out loud a story you'd written? Was it acting out plays with your friends? Was it trying to solve a practical problem?

After you've written what you can remember, sort your list into two groups: those that stifled your creativity and imagination and those that encouraged you to use your creativity and imagination. Note how those comments or instructions influenced your desire to develop your natural creativity as you grew older. Did you feel shut down? Did you feel inspired? What has your experience been with creativity since you were young? Are you ready to play with being creative now?

If you want to reconnect with earlier creativity in your life, move forward with your creativity, or explore some other ways to practice creativity, try these suggestions.

**Practice making imaginative mental connections between very different images.** For purely fun practice in using something specific for something else entirely, try making something with PVC pipe. This is a lightweight plastic pipe that can be found in the plumbing department of hardware or home improvement stores. A friend who was in charge of decorating a gym for a local charity's gala fundraising dinner used PVC pipe to create attractive supports for Japanese lanterns, hung all across the large ceiling. Spray painted black, the lightweight PVC pipe looked like elegant wrought iron holders. A quick Google search for "things to make with PVC pipe" revealed project ideas from a frame for a playhouse that fits inside a room to flower vases, wine racks, and bathtub toys. Are you trying to solve any problems or puzzles that could benefit from imagining connections between disparate objects? Play with ideas and see what you come up with. This creates the spark that gets our mental gears going so that we come up with a new idea or a new way of doing something.

**Practice looking at problems from different points of view to get a new perspective.** Our creativity is blocked when we are stuck thinking about a problem or an issue in just one way. When we practice viewing problems (and solutions) from multiple perspectives, we can avoid being blocked by the bias of our own assumptions. Here's where chapter 5's ideas on reframing and thinking in questions can be helpful. Ask yourself some of these questions: Am I looking at this as a *judger*? How can I look at this as a *learner*? How would someone with the opposite point of view describe this problem or envision a solution? When we can articulate an opposing point of view as well as the one we hold, the swirling of opposites often creates the conditions that spark a new point of view in our minds.

**Practice viewing problems or needs from the perspective of another profession.** Depending on what you are trying to accomplish, you might ask yourself: How would the coach of a soccer team approach this problem? Or how would a chef approach this problem? Or would a checklist help us improve what we do?

**Listen to your favorite music** when you are in pain or you feel overwhelmed, tired, depressed, stiff, or simply stuck in a rut. Let yourself be engaged with the rhythms, the tunes, the harmonies, the lyrics, or whatever you like best about the music.

Move to it if you can, so that you embody a physical, as well as emotional, response to the music.

**Explore the creative arts and find one you'd like to go deeper with.** Music, dance, pottery, woodworking, painting, pastels, drawing, theater, singing, writing, photography, textile art, design—these are just some of the things that can awaken your creativity and add enjoyment to your life.

**Stay play-nourished.** One of the quickest ways to jumpstart play is to do something physical. Just *move*. Take a walk, throw a ball for a dog, or dance to your favorite music. The important thing is to find the play that feeds your soul. It will also nourish your resilience.

Creativity is the energizer of resilience. When we use our imaginations to envision opportunities in our new reality, or to reframe our perspective, we are creating a spark that ignites our resilience. When we engage in creative activities, we are building our capacity for radical resilience by giving our attention and focus to something that is generative and life-affirming.

## Summary for Chapter 6: Creativity

### What is creativity as a radical resilience skill?

- A multifaceted skill that encompasses all the ways we use our imagination to see new ways to solve problems, do tasks, think new thoughts, understand new meanings, find a new use for something, or make something new.
- Much more than artistic ability.
- The ability to think of more than one possibility in response to a given idea, situation, or challenge.

## What are some ways to practice creativity?

- Making imaginative mental connections between very different images. For fun, practice using something specific for something else entirely.

- Listening to music and making music if we can. Music-making touches us in many ways. Try writing songs, singing with a group, playing an instrument.

- Staying play-nourished: puzzles, games, anything that's enjoyable to us.

- Exploring the creative arts.

- Experiment with various art forms: write, draw, play an instrument, sew, quilt, paint. Just play at first; if you want to go deeper with some, let that be later, when you know you like the medium and you want to take the next steps.

- Moving. Take a walk, dance to your favorite music, take up a sport, move just for fun.

# 7

# Realistic Optimism and Hope

P eople who have an optimistic, hopeful outlook on life recover from adversity better than people whose outlook on their situation is hopeless and pessimistic.[1] Studies show that this is true for a wide range of life's adversities, from being a prisoner of war to living with a life-threatening illness.[2] That's not to say that we'll engage our optimism and hope immediately after we've experienced an adverse event. As we've seen in many of the stories here, it's common at first to feel anxious, concerned, and even a little pessimistic about our future. It takes a certain amount of time to get our bearings and understand the reality of what's happened to us.

I use the term *realistic optimism*[3] in the context of radical resilience because it clarifies the difference between optimism and wishful thinking. Wishful thinking—the belief that something we want to have happen *will* happen, even though that's not likely or possible—is an obstacle to resilience. Wishful thinking that isn't intercepted and replaced by a realistic perspective can lead to delays, poor decisions, disillusionment, heartbreak, and despair. In contrast, *realistic optimism* is a combination of optimism, which is thinking from a positive perspective, and pessimism, which is thinking from a negative perspective. The mix of optimism and pessimism minimizes the disadvantages of being overly optimistic by including an assessment from the negative side of the situation. Yet at the same time, the energy that's generated by seeing the positive side helps to overcome the discouragement engendered by the negative assessment.[4]

When we engage both optimism and pessimism in our response to adversity, we're building *realistic optimism*. It's a powerful resilience skill because we're engaging opposite traits at the same time—a known factor in the capacity to adapt to new conditions.[5]

Hope adds action to realistic optimism. I used to think of hope as simply being one aspect of a positive attitude. But C. R. Snyder found that hope actually engages us in action. A pioneer in the study of hope, Snyder found that in addition to having the quality of a positive attitude, hope has three other elements: setting a goal we want to attain, envisioning possible ways to reach that goal, and taking specific steps along one or more of those ways toward attaining our goal.[6] This process can take a while, especially if our recovery time is expected to be lengthy, as it was for Jill Taylor, in chapter 3. In that case, it works well to keep a long-range goal in mind but also to plan a series of short-term goals that we can accomplish one at a time. As we experience the satisfaction of reaching our smaller goals, we'll either be able to see the possibility of reaching our long-range goal or we may see that an alternative goal would be better. In either case, hope and realistic optimism together help us meet adverse challenges with radical resilience. They engage us in taking stock of our situation, setting short-term and long-term goals, planning small steps we can take toward attaining these goals, and taking those steps as soon as we're able.

My friend Steven's experience is an example of how realistic optimism and hope work together as resilience skills. Wiry, athletic, and in his forties, Steven ruptured his Achilles tendon while playing volleyball one evening after work. Friends took him to the hospital where, after several hours, he ended up with a heavy cast on his left leg. Steven took his hospital experience in stride until the doctor gave him discharge instructions and told him the prognosis. The doctor said he must not put any weight at all on that leg for at least six weeks. In addition, the complete healing of his Achilles tendon would probably take a year or more. Finally, the worst news—there was a big chance that Steven might not ever be able to play volleyball again.

Steven went home from the hospital, tired, hurting, discouraged, and depressed. For the first few days after his accident, he was irritable, self-consumed, and worried about how he would be able to carry on his life of college teaching and vigorous physical activities. At times his pain was excruciating. An avid hiker and bicycle commuter as well as volleyball enthusiast, he couldn't imagine how he could be himself if he had to be sedentary for weeks on end. All he could picture were long months of inactivity and boredom.

Although Steven had overcome many personal challenges in his life, he'd never been faced with one that stopped him physically. At first he fretted about how he could manage. He wanted to be as independent as possible during his recovery, but he didn't know how to proceed. As he took stock of his situation, it became clear to him that he'd do better with a less fretful attitude. So he began to think creatively about what he needed and wanted. He talked with friends, and friends of friends, who had experienced mobility limitations. New ideas and resources emerged.

Within a few days, his gloomy attitude was gone. Hope and realistic optimism took its place. Steven found a store that rented mobility devices designed specifically for people with leg injuries. A bright red, non-motorized scooter was a perfect solution, and he was soon very mobile. The scooter empowered his active inner spirit by freeing him from the sense of awkwardness and vulnerability he'd felt using crutches. Steven was thrilled to demonstrate the wonder of his new "wheels." He cruised by my office the afternoon he got it and called to me to come outside. As he skidded to a stop in front of me, he shouted with a grin, "I'm going to make it!"

Steven's friends would probably say that he's a naturally optimistic and hopeful person, so it isn't surprising that his optimism surfaced when he faced adversity. But as soon as the shock of being confined to inactivity wore off and his pain became manageable, he didn't simply have an *attitude* of hope and optimism—he *engaged* his hope and optimism to find ways to move forward toward his goal of being as independent as possible.

First, he decided to be positive rather than fretful about his situation. Then, in looking realistically at his situation, he questioned the assumption that the only way he could get around on one leg was on crutches. Could this assumption be an *unnecessary limitation?* He decided to talk with people he knew who'd had similar experiences and ask for their advice about resources. That's how he learned about the scooters. He found one, tried it, and was restored to his confident, capable self.

Steven engaged in this process of hopeful, realistic optimism the moment he decided that he wanted to be as independent as possible during the weeks he couldn't put any weight on his leg. He set some goals to find out how he could reach a better level of independence than his crutches allowed. Getting the non-motorized scooter helped him meet his goal of increased independence and gave him renewed emotional as well as physical energy.

From that point on, Steven progressed through the rigors of rehabilitation. That he could so joyously say, "I'm going to make it," even in the very early stages of his rehabilitation therapy, shows how he engaged realistic optimism and hope together to get a handle on how he was going to live for the unknown span of his disability. Steven was fortunate that his injury would only seriously incapacitate him for six weeks and moderately incapacitate him for about a year. After that, he could expect to return to active sports, and, he hoped, even to volleyball.

When we're challenged by life-changing limitations, times of despair and worry may appear more than once in the process of a resilient recovery. When we name them, face them, and desire to overcome them, we engage the resilience skills and begin to adapt to the changes imposed on us.

Richard Cohen, author and journalist, has lived with multiple sclerosis (MS) for over forty years. I first learned about him when I read *Blindsided*, his memoir about living with MS and later of undergoing treatment for colon cancer.[7] The memoir's subtitle, *Lifting a Life above Illness*, illustrates the radical resilience that Cohen learned to exhibit as he lived with a severe form of this unpredictable disease of the central nervous system. After forty-one years of living with MS, Cohen writes, "MS is all about things you can't do anymore. Things you have to give up. And I just think you have to fight on one hand and be realistic on the other."[8]

Research suggests that individuals with high hope are more confident that they can generate pathways to reach desired goals than their low-hope counterparts.[9] But what about high hopes or unrealistic expectations? Won't it be a problem if we get our hopes up but then things don't work out as we had hoped they would? Not necessarily, say David Feldman and Maximilian Kubota. Getting our hopes up won't expose us to any greater failure or disappointment than not hoping at all. In contrast, they say, "Hopeful thinking appears to increase the probability of successfully accomplishing goals."[10]

My brother, a retired surgeon who served many cancer patients, found that hopeful thinking is very important in a person's recovery. When patients used to ask him, "How long do I have, doctor?" he would first tell them the percentage of people with their condition who had lived the longest amount of time (say, twenty years.) Then he would tell them the percentage that had lived the shortest amount of time (say, six months). And then he'd say, "Right now, there's no reason that you can't be in the twenty-year group."

Research supports his view that having a hopeful attitude and optimistic view is as important to the patient's outcome as knowing the prognosis. A 2011 study of cardiac patients at Duke University Medical Center found that those with optimistic expectations of recovery were more likely to survive over the next fifteen years than the less hopeful patients.[11]

Although some people seem to be naturally optimistic, many of us tend to see the negative aspects of life more immediately and clearly than the positive ones. It's not that we are pessimistic by nature; it's that we believe that honesty about the downsides or risks of situations or decisions is important. Happiness research expert Sonya Lyubomirsky agrees that being optimistic doesn't mean denying the negative or avoiding all unfavorable information. And it doesn't mean constantly trying to control situations that cannot be controlled. In fact, she writes, research shows that realistic (she uses the word "flexible") optimists are *more*, not less, vigilant of risks and threats because they don't have their blinders on. Realistic, or flexible, optimists are also very much aware that positive outcomes are dependent on their efforts. Thus, they participate in making their situation better and don't wait around for good things to happen.[12]

Even though realistic optimism incorporates an awareness of the negatives involved in a situation, it does not emphasize them. When we're being realistically optimistic, we balance the negative factors with the positive factors, and we proceed with a hopeful attitude toward the best possible outcome. Unlike an optimism based on fantasy that ignores the negative aspects of the situation, realistic optimism considers all the facts and chooses to look toward a positive outcome.

If we lean toward a pessimistic way of looking at the world, are we always going to be poor candidates for resilience when life's challenges overwhelm us and we want to give up? No, says Martin Seligman in his book *Learned Optimism*.[13] We can choose to turn around our pessimistic way of interpreting our world and replace it with a more optimistic one.

Both realistic optimism and hope are active—not passive—attitudes. They are attitudes that empower us to take initiatives toward recovery from any event that results in life-changing limitations, whether temporary or permanent. Setting small goals, reaching them, evaluating the results, setting the next goals—this is the process of both realistic optimism and hope.

Sometimes our goals will be specific steps that get us through a waiting period or a treatment regimen—those times in which we don't know how things are going to turn out. We need small steps to support our sense of self during those difficult times. I have a friend who recently had a diagnosis of cancer that required an initial twenty-eight-day regimen of chemotherapy treatments before surgery. She decided to buy twenty-eight pieces of her favorite, very expensive, chocolate as a treat at the end of each day of treatment. She didn't buy a ready-made box of chocolates because she knew there were certain pieces in every box that she didn't enjoy. So she went to her favorite candy shop, handpicked twenty-eight pieces, and had them packed in a special box. Not only did each piece serve as a reward at the end of each treatment day but the disappearing pieces were a visual sign that the days of treatment were diminishing. Her friends and family cheered her on, as at the end of each day we got an email report of how her treatment was progressing and which piece of chocolate she had just enjoyed.

Sometimes we have to make changes in our social network if we are to be supported in our efforts to practice realistic optimism and hope. A friend told a story of a woman who had been through terrible difficulties. The woman realized that she had to make a conscious decision to surround herself with optimistic people rather than pessimistic, negative ones. She realized that when she was among her negative acquaintances, she would get depressed and hopeless herself, but when she was among those with a more positive and hopeful outlook on life in general and on their own lives in particular, she felt much better. When considering her situation from a hopeful, real- istically optimistic perspective, she developed new friendships so she could have a friendship network that would help her maintain her newfound positive outlook on life. Friends and colleagues have told me similar stories. Lyubomirsky writes that if friends put us down or make us feel miserable, we need to find friends who are more helpful.[14] It's important to have supporters who are optimistic and hopeful.

Steven, with his torn Achilles tendon, set goals to get him through his recovery period. So did my friend in preparation for her chemotherapy, and many of the others here. Realistic optimism and hope, along with mindfulness and courage and other resilience skills, provide the strong foundation that supports our capacity for resilience. And resilience gives us new life when unpredictable events challenge our sense of self and stop us from being the person we were—and doing the things that gave our lives meaning—before the events occurred.

## Some Ways to Practice Realistic Optimism and Hope

Other resilience skills can help us turn our initial tendency toward pessimism into an increasing capacity for realistic optimism. Reframing, flexibility, and creativity are particularly helpful in building our capacity for realistic optimism. They offer many approaches to setting aside our assumptions and looking at things differently.

Practice reframing. We can ask ourselves, "How can I reframe this situation so that I see something positive?" That's the question that Susan asked herself when the house deal fell through (chapter 5). She was amazed at the result—a release from fearful anxiety and a newfound confidence in her ability to move forward. My friend who chose twenty-eight favorite chocolates asked herself, "What can I do to make this experience better?

What can I do that will give me something to look forward to during this difficult time?"

**Practice flexibility.** We can identify something we have fixed ideas about or are fearful of and explore those realities from the perspective of an openminded, positive outlook. If, for example, we're adamant about living in our own home until we die, we might talk with people who have chosen other senior living options and visit some places that might be possible options *if* we couldn't live safely in our own home any longer. Since we're just exploring for the sake of developing flexibility and realistic optimism, it doesn't matter if we find the "ideal" place or not. What matters is that we've looked at something we wouldn't consider before and enlarged our sphere of possibility should a life-changing limitation occur. Then, if the time comes that we need to move, our attitude will shift from "I'll never leave my home" to "this alternative might work."

**Practice creativity.** Creative thinking and creative activity have a lot of power to replace a pessimistic outlook with a realistically optimistic one. Listening to a piece of music that we enjoy or playing an instrument we love can usually bring us into a more optimistic frame of mind and heart. Or we might explore expressing our feelings through music, art, movement, or writing. If we're psychologically oriented, we might want to take on our pessimism as an adversary and find out just why we are stuck in it.

**Engage with spirituality.** Trust is an important aspect of our ability to maintain realistic optimism and hope. When we face the hard work of responding to adversity, one of the first realizations is that we're not in control. Instead, we're in the midst of uncertainty, when nothing is clear about what to do and how to do it. Having a reliable set of spiritual practices that help us connect with sources of spiritual strength helps us be hopeful and at the same time realistic about our situation. Practices such as prayer or meditation that connect us with a source of trust and spiritual guidance are crucial to radical resilience. It takes courage to face the realities of adversity and trust that we will know when to accept or when to reject the solutions that are offered by the professionals in charge. It takes spiritual strength to surrender control so our higher power can work within us.

Realistic optimism and hope are grounded in courage, a will to live, and a desire to take an active part in the process of recovery from adversity. Although they require us to face the truth about our situation, they also empower us to set realistic goals and actively work to reach them. Along with the other resilience skills, realistic optimism and hope help us to grow in self-awareness and our ability to live with a sense of well-being, even amid uncertainty.

## Summary for Chapter 7: Realistic Optimism and Hope

### What is realistic optimism as a radical resilience skill?

- A mix of optimism and pessimism.
- Takes into account the negatives of a situation but gives the positives of the situation more weight and importance.

### What are some ways to practice realistic optimism?

- Practicing reframing.

  - Asking, "How can I reframe this situation so that I see something positive?" or "What can I do that will give me something to look forward to during this difficult time?"

- Practicing flexibility.

  - Looking ahead to what we might need to deal with and finding ways to adapt to the realities of our situation before they are forced on us.
  - Examine alternatives.

- Practicing creativity.

  - Creative thinking and creative activity have a lot of power to replace a pessimistic outlook with a realistically optimistic one.
  - Being as physically active as we can. This will boost our morale and help us feel better.

- Practicing spirituality.

  - Connect with our sources of spiritual strength.
  - Engage with spiritual practices that support our mind/body/spirit connection.

## What is hope as a radical resilience skill?

- A positive attitude, a goal, a vision of possible ways to reach that goal, and taking specific steps to reach it.
- Hope adds action to realistic optimism.

## What are some ways to practice hope?

- Focusing on what we can control; then developing preliminary goals that will help us reach our end goal.

  - Identifying small steps we can take to reach each of our preliminary goals and taking them.
  - Celebrating each step we take.

- Following this process until we reach our end goal.

- Remembering to adjust our goals according to the reality of our life.

  ○ Sometimes it will take longer to reach the preliminary goals than we anticipate.

- Practicing reframing, flexibility, creativity, spirituality, and physical activity along with hope. They support and enhance one another.

# 8

# Physical Activity

P hysical activity is a resilience skill? Yes—absolutely.
Physical activity and exercise improve mood, reduce
symptoms of depression and anxiety, increase functional
capacity, and change our brain in ways that protect our memory and our thinking skills.[1] All these benefits are important
for resilience—and especially for *radical* resilience. Physical
activity and exercise are good for our brains as well as for
our bodies, for our emotions as well as for our overall sense
of well-being. What's the difference between them? Physical
activity is movement that is carried out by our skeletal muscles and requires energy. Exercise is planned, structured, repet-
itive, and intentional movement that is intended to improve or
maintain physical fitness. It is a subset of physical activity. Even
small amounts of exercise, such as a short walk, can recharge
our energy and stimulate our creativity.[2]

Avoiding regular physical activity is very dangerous behavior. The World Health Organization (WHO) has identified
physical *inactivity* as an independent risk factor for chronic
disease development. In fact, physical inactivity, also known as
sedentary behavior, is now the fourth leading cause of death
worldwide.[3] If we don't engage in moderate to vigorous exercise
or physical activity most days of the week, our bodies and our

brains go into decline. It is as simple as that. Too much sitting can kill us.[4]

There are many reasons that we don't engage in enough physical activity to keep our bodies and minds as well as we'd like them to be. Here are five common barriers that discourage us from engaging in physical activities and exercise:

**Functional limitations that make exercise difficult or painful.** These drain our courage and create a fear of pain, of falling, or of feeling worse than we do now. Jill's stroke-related functional limitations (chapter 3) were a barrier to physical activity and exercise. But she overcame them by persevering with her practice of walking with weights, over and over again for more than three years despite the ungainliness of an awkward gait, until she mastered the ability to walk with a smooth gait again.

**Low energy, fatigue, or a generally depressed mood.** These can snuff out our desire or our good intentions to move more and be more physically active.

**A preference for sedentary activities.** Reading, knitting, sewing, writing, playing computer games, or chatting with friends on the phone or through the internet can override our interest in physical activity and usurp the thirty minutes we might have spent in more active movement.

**An entrenched habit of inactivity.** Such a habit is not only difficult to overcome, it can lead to a subtle but dangerous belief that we cannot change—that being physically active, or engaging in an exercise program, is something we'll *never* be able to do. I have several friends who have been using walkers, wheelchairs, or electric scooters for basic mobility because of painful arthritic joints in their lower body. At first these devices were very helpful. But over time they displaced each person's ability to walk comfortably without them. One friend has stopped walking on her own. I've noticed that now, when she starts to sit down on a chair, she falls into it. Because her leg and lower body muscles are too weak to support her body, she can no longer ease her body into a chair. I suspect that unless she begins to strengthen those muscles, she'll lose her ability to walk even a few steps without help.

**Learned helplessness.** Identified by Martin Seligman, learned helplessness is the reaction we have when we switch into an attitude of passivity because we believe that there's nothing we can do to change our situation.[5] In relation to physical activity, learned helplessness can occur in situations like the one above, where my friend has used ambulation devices for so long that she's afraid to walk at all without one. She's not interested in physical therapy to help her walk again because she believes it won't help her. But learned helplessness can also be forced upon residents of nursing homes and other assisted care settings. Sometimes this is because operational efficiency is valued over holistic attention to the needs of the residents.[6] It also may be due to lack of awareness at the management level that strength training and other exercise are beneficial to people of all ages. Therefore, no effort is made in those settings to hire trained staff to guide and support people in ongoing, restorative exercise.

An older relative of mine—I'll call her Irene—used a wheelchair to get around her home after she hurt her foot. A stroke had resulted in some left-side impairment several years before, and she used a walker for steadiness. Irene was happy to have the wheelchair to use while her foot recovered.

However, since it was so much easier to get around her house in the wheelchair, she continued to use it long after her foot healed. She got to where she was afraid to be without it. Irene was able to get up and move around in the kitchen or transfer to a chair in the dining room or living room, but she lost her confidence for walking more than a few steps by herself. Suggestions that she walk behind the wheelchair, so that she'd strengthen her legs but have the wheelchair available if she needed it, didn't make sense to her. After a year, she'd lost so much strength in her core muscles and legs that she couldn't walk independently, even with a walker.

Irene moved to a new assisted care facility with the hope of improving her ability to walk so that she could return to her home. This assisted living facility advertised a water exercise program that was particularly appealing to her. The admitting staff and Irene all knew that Irene needed help to transfer from the wheelchair to the pool for water exercise. But after she'd moved in, it turned out that the activity staff person was not licensed to handle this type of transfer. No effort was ever made to find a way to help Irene with leg-strengthening exercise.

After a while, Irene decided to practice walking on her own by holding on to a rail that ran along the hallway wall. A nurse saw her holding on tight to the rail and struggling to stand up. The nurse ran over to Irene. Instead of helping Irene stand and walk, the nurse chastised her for making the attempt and insisted that she sit right down in the wheelchair.

"Don't do that again," the nurse told Irene. "We don't want you to fall." As a result, Irene stayed wheelchair-bound for more than a year. She tried to make the best of the situation, but she became depressed. "I came here to get better," she said, "but I can see now that I'll never be able to go home." She gave up believing she would ever be able to walk again—even with the help of a walker.

## Catalysts for Change: Four Stories

### Irene's story, continued

The following year, Irene moved to another state to live with a daughter. There, she participated in an innovative program that first assessed her potential to improve her physical functioning and then engaged her in therapeutic physical exercise to strengthen her legs and her core muscles.[7] Irene worked hard at the exercises. In just three months, she was able to walk with her walker. She never used the wheelchair for general mobility again, even after a tough recovery from colon cancer surgery. Irene's ability to walk with a walker for the rest of her life increased her functional capacity and her sense of well-being. The wheelchair came out only on the occasions of a trip to the mall for shopping or lunch, where the crowds and the distances made using the wheelchair a better choice than managing with a walker.

Having the proper professional support was crucial for Irene's recovery of her ability to walk. This, in turn, led to the restoration of her sense of self and her enjoyment of life.

### Andrew Solomon's story

In his memoir, *The Noonday Demon: An Atlas of Depression*, Solomon describes why, even in the midst of clinical depression, he became determined to overcome his resistance to exercise:

> . . . depression makes your body heavy and sluggish; and being heavy and sluggish exacerbates depression. If you keep

making your body function, as much as you can, your mind will follow suit. A really serious workout is just about the most disgusting idea I can imagine when I'm depressed, and it's no fun doing it, but afterward I always feel a thousand times better. Exercise allays anxiety too: nervous energy gets used up by sit-ups, and this helps to contain irrational fear.[8]

## Marie's story

My friend Marie says that her heart attack was the wake-up call that motivated her to get started with exercise. Before her heart attack, she had been a busy person who felt that her normal comings and goings were sufficient activity. Like many of us, she confused being busy with being active. Regular exercise seemed like a chore. After work and on weekends, Marie liked to relax by reading a good book or watching TV while she worked on her current knitting or quilting projects. She'd always disliked the thought of building a specific exercise program into her life.

Then the heart attack happened. "I realized with a shock that this heart attack had almost ended my life." She decided to participate wholeheartedly in the cardiac rehabilitation program that her doctor recommended. Once she made that decision, she never looked back. She learned how to exercise properly, how to evaluate her exertion level, and how to monitor her body's response to exercise. Gradually, she overcame her resistance to building an intentional exercise time into her life. She also joined a yoga class and found she enjoyed it.

After about six months, Marie noticed that she felt better than she'd felt for several years. She'd lost her excess weight, felt much more energetic, slept better at night, and no longer needed to take blood pressure medicine. Now, several years later, she would not give up her exercise regimen for anything. "Exercise has made a huge difference for me. Now I know how important it is for my life. And only I can do it for myself. Nobody else—and no pills—can do it for me. Besides, I actually like it now. Can you believe it?" Marie is unusual. Studies have shown that people who've experienced a life-changing medical event like a heart attack or stroke and who've been told by their doctors to exercise more still don't manage to build it into their lives. Even people who'd exercised regularly before the medical event often don't continue with exercise in the reality of their changed lives.[9] Marie's story illustrates the value of exercise as a radical resilience skill that can be started at any time and practiced intentionally for the rest of our lives. The benefits to our health and well-being are well worth the effort.

## Bill's story

Bill, who'd been a swimmer for many years, stopped being physically active when a serious illness led to the amputation of both his legs.[10] Bill thought that swimming would be impossible without his legs. A transformative moment about two years after his amputation sparked his desire to overcome his limitations and swim again. While he was on a vacation, he'd come upon a beautiful cove, with sea water gently flowing into it. Stirred deeply by the scene, Bill knew that he wanted to swim there someday. Right then he vowed that he'd investigate swimming at his local pool when he returned home.

On his first visit to his local pool, not sure of how things were arranged, Bill took his two artificial limbs off in the changing room and put them in a locker. Then he crawled to the poolside and rolled in. He'd already decided that once he surfaced, he would just move his arms and see what happened. Very quickly, Bill realized that he'd need to relearn how to swim. "The first time I went along to the pool, I only managed a couple of lengths and I was absolutely exhausted. But this did not deter me and I gradually built up my lengths and got so much stronger."

Following the initial visit when he'd crawled to the poolside, Bill tried many different ways of getting into the water, including the poolside hoist. He finally concluded that he preferred using the hoist to anything else. Staff became aware of Bill's needs and offered him a wheelchair to use from the changing rooms to the poolside hoist. That helped a lot.

Bill retaught himself how to swim during the public swim session, and after eleven months he'd finally mastered the front crawl again. He'd also gained other benefits, for during those months of swim practice Bill's overall fitness, mobility, and breathing improved. He lost fifty-six pounds and his stumps became softer and less painful. After a while he stepped up into a leadership role at the pool by becoming a *"swim buddy"*—a support person for new and apprehensive adult swimmers.

Bill's story also illustrates the use of other resilience skills. The scene at the cove was a *spiritual* experience that gave him the inspiration and desire to swim again. He showed *the courage to be vulnerable* not only by being willing to be seen in a public pool, but also when he overcame embarrassment and discomfort as he crawled from the changing room to the pool, and later, when he accepted help from the staff.

He showed *perseverance and creativity* as he figured out, by trial and error, the best way to get into and out of the water after he reached the pool's edge. He showed *perseverance and courage* in working for eleven months until he could really swim again.

Bill used the skill of *reframing* in at least three ways: first, he looked at his situation through a new frame when the cove gave him a reason to swim again; second, he let go of his assumption that he couldn't swim without legs and decided to try; and third, he approached the task of relearning to swim from a learner mindset. He asked the questions that would help him figure out his next steps. He explored different ways to accomplish those steps. *Mindfulness* kept him focused on his goal. *Flexibility* and *creativity* led him to think of new ways to meet his goals. *Realistic optimism* helped him stay aware of what he could and could not do along the way. *Hope* kept him focused on his progress and strengthened his belief that his goal of swimming again was indeed possible. The *physical activity* he engaged in throughout his process served him well to strengthen his body, ease the pain of his stumps, and restore a part of his life that he thought he'd never have back. And *spirituality* lies at the heart of the compassion Bill showed in being a swim buddy for adults who were afraid of getting into the water.

## The Power of Habit

A preference for sedentary activities and an entrenched habit of inactivity are both obstacles that I face in trying to build regular exercise and physical activity into my life. When I read Charles Duhigg's *The Power of Habit: Why We Do What We Do in Life and Business*, about how habits are formed and how we can change them, I knew I'd found an important resource

for overcoming my habit of avoiding much physical activity.
I liked Duhigg's explanation of steps to take to analyze and
change an unwanted habit. After summarizing his approach to
changing an unwanted habit, I'll show how his book helped
me to change mine.

According to Duhigg, every habit has three components:
a cue, a routine, and a reward.[11] The cue triggers an action (a
routine) that results in something that satisfies us (a reward).
Duhigg describes how he changed his work habit of going to
the cafeteria every afternoon and buying a cookie. His cue:
the moment he sensed the desire for a pleasurable break from
work. His routine: getting up from his desk and walking to the
cafeteria. His reward: eating a delicious cookie. After identifying the cue and the routine, he made a plan to try alternative
routines and rewards.

As Duhigg experimented with different rewards and routines, and as he paid attention to the cue's context, he discovered that the urge to get up and get a cookie came between
three and four in the afternoon. He also discovered, after
exploring several different rewards and routines, that although
he liked the cookie, the main reward he sought from his afternoon break was socialization. Since several other people on
his floor also enjoyed taking a break at that time, Duhigg discovered that he could fulfill his need by having an informal
conversation without going to the cafeteria. If nobody on his
floor was free to chat, he'd still go to the cafeteria, get a cup of
tea (a different reward), and find someone who'd enjoy a chat
while he drank his tea. Either of those two different routines/
rewards satisfied him. After either one, he returned to his desk
energized, satisfied, and glad that he was free from a habit he
didn't want.

## How Duhigg's Process Worked for Me

I decided to use Duhigg's process to break my deeply entrenched habit of inactivity. As I isolated the cue and identified my reward, I realized that my reward was embedded in my preference for sedentary behavior. *I liked not exercising.* For years, because I knew it was good for me, I'd made attempts to include intentional exercise into my life. But none of them wore well with me. They didn't hold my interest and I didn't experience any rewards. So over time they weren't sustainable.

However, I hadn't ever realized that sedentary behavior is harmful. I usually move around quite a bit in my daily life, and I believed that was enough. Like Marie, I assumed that being busy with daily activities was as good as focused exercise. But for me, it wasn't. I was going from room to room, or cubicle to cubicle—not gardening or doing heavy cleaning or anything physically vigorous that required endurance. To interrupt the decline in my mobility, I needed to break my habit of inactivity and replace it with a habit of engaging in regular physical activity at least five days a week.

Although I paid attention to the steps in Duhigg's process, my process was a little different. First, I thought about my reward—avoidance of vigorous exercise. My new awareness that sedentary behavior is deadly made me realize that I needed a different perspective on the value of no exercise. So I worked on reframing my preference for sedentary behavior. It wasn't long before I came to understand that a preference for sedentary behavior is just that—a *preference.* Furthermore, now that I realized that sedentary behavior for too many hours is harmful, not exercising was no longer a reward I wanted. Instead, I wanted regular physical activity that I could enjoy, that I could afford, and, at the end of the day, that I could recognize as contributing to my health and well-being.

I then examined the routines I'd previously done when deciding to exercise. None of them had worked for long. So I tried something different—water exercise, three mornings a week. I didn't mind the drive and the changing clothes as much as I thought I would. And after the first week, I realized that I felt better and could move much better on the days after I'd been to the water exercise class. Later, I filled in the other two weekdays with an exercise class designed to strengthen the core muscles and stretch everything else.

Now, a year after starting water exercise, I feel incomplete at the end of the day if I haven't been able to exercise at least forty-five minutes during the day. I feel more energetic throughout the day when I exercise, and I can walk with a spring in my step without stiffness or pain. I'm stronger now too. My reward has become the opposite of what it was—*I like how I feel* after I've exercised. Although I still enjoy sedentary activities such as reading or working at the computer, I also like the physical activities I now practice. In fact, on the days that I don't participate in those activities, I miss the sense of emotional and physical well-being that I experience when I do them.

**We *can* overcome the habit of inactivity.** To do this, though, we need first to delve deep into ourselves and identify a motivation for why we want to do it. Irene wanted to walk more but she needed an environment that could support her in strengthening her muscles so that she *could* walk again. Once she had that supportive environment, she was able to do the work that would restore her functioning.

Marie's motivation came from her deep realization that a heart attack had almost killed her. Once she had a second chance at life, she was determined to exercise regularly in order to live longer. Andrew's motivation was that he felt so much better after he exercised. So even though he described the very *idea* of exercising first thing in the morning as "*disgusting*," he did it anyway. And he's glad he did because he feels better than ever.

Bill's motivation came from seeing a cove where he wanted to swim someday. My motivation continues to come from not wanting to lose my independence or my ability to go places. I don't want to lose my mobility and I don't want to slide into learned helplessness. And when I saw that was happening and learned that sedentary behavior is deadly, I was able to change course and see exercise and physical activity from a different perspective.

Without an inner reason that compels us to keep working on building a habit of regular exercise, good intentions and sporadic exercise will prevail. Duhigg's approach to overcoming the power of an entrenched habit can be used as he describes, or it can be adapted, as I did, to fit our situation.

I found that in the process of identifying cues and experimenting with different routines and rewards, I was using several radical resilience skills. I've incorporated some *mindfulness* techniques into my water exercise program by working on focus, centering, and enjoying the feel of the water around my body. I began to *reframe* regular exercise as being something I enjoy and that enhances my life and sense of well-being—it's no longer something I have to do because someone else says it's good for me. I continue to use *realistic optimism* as I adjust to the reality of the conflicts that prevent my participation in the water exercise or core strengthening programs, and figure out other ways to get in thirty minutes or more of intentional physical activity into my daily life wherever I am.

## Some Ways to Practice Physical Activity

- Consult with your doctor before engaging in any new exercise or physical activity.
- List the physical activities that you *like* and *can do;* then choose something from your list to do at least five days of the week.
- Get up and move whenever you can.
- For cardiovascular benefit, perform activity in bouts of at least ten minutes duration. Try for a total of 30–60 minutes a day on most days of the week.
- Dance or exercise to music in your home.
- Take a walk most days of the week.
- Write your physical activity plan on your calendar and do it.
- Make a contingency plan for bad weather.
- Break up long periods of sitting as often as possible.
- Exercise with a friend.
- Do tasks around the home that require lifting, carrying, or digging.
- Join a gym and work with weights or other resistance training.
- See the resources section at the end of this book for rescources on physical activity. You'll find websites and print materials that are inspiring and instructional about physical activity and exercise that we can do without special equipment or in a gym.

Physical activity and exercise are critically important for our health, our capacity to function mentally as well as physically, our sense of well-being, our level of mental and physical energy, and our ability to respond to life's changes and challenges with radical resilience. So whatever our specific health conditions are, we will benefit from daily practice of this simple motto: Sit less. Move more.

## Summary for Chapter 8: Physical Activity

### What are physical activity and exercise as radical resilience skills?

- Ways to improve mood, reduce symptoms of depression and anxiety, increase functional capacity, and change our brains in ways that protect our memory and our thinking skills.

### What are some ways to practice physical activity?

- Overcoming the habit of inactivity if we have it.
- Using the other resilience skills to help us choose to engage in exercise or other physical activity for at least the minimum weekly level that our doctor says is appropriate and beneficial for us.
- Planning how we will exercise regularly.
- Having plans for good and bad weather.
- Scheduling our physical activity a week at a time, and writing it in our calendar.
  - If we need to change our plan, finding an alternate way to meet our physical activity goal for the week.
- Sit less. Move more.

# 9

# Spirituality

think of spirituality as our connection with the transcendent spiritual power of life. This power is beyond comprehension yet is knowable through our own inner spirit. We call that mystery by many different names. Whether we think of this spiritual power as God, Higher Power, Great Mystery, Great Spirit, Life Force, Deep Reality Within, or another name, our own spirituality develops when we desire to have a relationship with it. Most of us develop our relationship with this spiritual power through practices such as prayer, meditation, or ritual.

Spirituality lies at the heart of our search for meaning, purpose, and direction in life. It speaks to our need to be aligned with something bigger than our physical being. Spirituality fulfills our desire for a life that has meaning beyond ourselves. It lives in our desire for love, for inner growth, for deeper consciousness, and for inner peace. It lives in our sense of connectedness with nature, other people, and the world around us. It also lives in our desire to make a positive difference in the world. Whenever we aren't satisfied with only the material side of life and we feel the urge for *something more*, that's a door into spirituality.[1]

Attending to our spirituality is an essential skill for radical resilience. The kinds of challenges and adversities in life that demand radical resilience usually cause pain and suffering. We cannot handle pain and suffering without spiritual support. Much of that spiritual support will come from people—some from those we know and some from strangers who offer a kind word or come forward to help when we need it. We might also find spiritual support through our religious tradition, twelve-step program, or a meditative practice such as tai chi, mindfulness meditation, or yoga.

However, not all religions or spiritual belief systems are helpful for radical resilience. Any religion or spiritual belief system that is judgmental, punitive, rigid, or exclusive is a potential obstacle to resilience. The kind of spirituality that serves as a radical resilience skill respects the dignity of every human being; understands that all beings, the environment, and the universe are interconnected; views the Higher Power as loving; and holds honesty, self-awareness, compassion, forgiveness, reconciliation, openness, acceptance, and healing as core values.

Whenever we seek to understand how we can best live our lives with meaning and purpose, through prayer, meditation, or other practice of spiritual discernment, and we pay attention with an open mind to what comes to us in response to that practice, we're engaging with our spirituality as a radical resilience skill. Over time, engagement with spirituality in this way is transformative. It changes the way we understand ourselves. It opens our hearts to an awareness of gratitude and leads us into greater compassion and a sense of connection with others.

Spirituality doesn't protect us from experiencing dark times; instead, it sustains and strengthens us during those times and helps us get through them. Matthew Fox writes that spirituality does not make us otherworldly; it makes us more alive.[2] Spirituality ultimately leads us from "who we thought we were" to a more humble yet fuller, deeper, richer sense of ourselves and of our relationship with others. We cannot grow in our inner life, nor respond to life's adversities with radical resilience, without it.

Matt Sanford found that yoga changed his life years after he'd become paralyzed from the chest down and confined to a wheelchair. He tells his story in *Waking: A Memoir of Trauma and Transcendence.*[3] Toward the close of his story, he writes:

> Healing can travel in so many directions. . . . Barring some sort of miracle, I am never going to walk again. More to the point, my body has sustained a lot of damage, and it is never going to be easy to live in. . . . Yoga definitely helps. It makes me feel better not just physically, not just mentally, but it helps me feel the core of my existence. . . . But without these difficulties, I would not be who I am. . . . There is still so much to realize. My experience tells me that the silence within us can be experienced energetically as a nourishing spa. When this happens, consciousness changes shape.[4]

Research shows that spirituality and religiosity often serve as buffers to the stresses of numerous diseases such as bipolar disorder, diabetes, heart disease, cancer, visual impairment, and HIV.[5] Often, the onset of a life-threatening disease is a catalyst that engages us deeply with our spirituality. A health crisis forces us to confront issues of pain, suffering, our life's purpose, and the reality of what has happened to us. In one study, cancer patients reported their spirituality helped them find hope, gratitude, and positivity in their cancer experience; they found that spirituality was a source of strength that helped them cope, find meaning in their lives, and make sense of the cancer experience all the way through the recovery from their treatment.[6]

I first experienced spirituality's role in radical resilience when I was in my late thirties. A large lawn mower blocked my path as I pulled into the garage one autumn day in 1975. When I leaned over to move it out of my way, a burning pain shot down my right leg. I gasped at the power of the pain and barely managed to get into the house. Almost unable to move, I collapsed on the living room sofa. A month earlier I'd learned that my unborn child of four months had died *in utero* and I was in the sad position, on doctor's orders, of waiting for my body to miscarry naturally. So I was not in the best of conditions, physical or emotional, to handle this new problem. As I lay on the sofa that afternoon, I had no idea that this was the first day of six months of relentless pain, immobility, and growing depression. I also didn't know that this time of pain, loss, and suffering would forge a spiritual path in my soul like a river forges its path through hard rock.

When after several days I was still in pain and even less able to move, I again called my obstetrician. He had prescribed pain medication for me earlier and it wasn't helping much. I'd called this time to ask how much sherry I could safely drink while taking the pain meds. "If you're asking me that question, I think you should be in the hospital," he said. Then, after asking a few diagnostic questions, he told me to call an ambulance.

There were strong winds and heavy rain that day, and the small town's ambulance was already in service. My husband called a neighbor and together they managed to get me into the back seat of our VW camper where I could lie flat for the thirty-mile trip. I learned later that my face was ashen when I arrived, and the emergency team that met me at the hospital door was concerned for my life.

After some days had passed, neurological tests revealed that my right leg and foot were paralyzed. The doctors thought that the cause could be the uterus pressing on the spine, so now there was a medical reason to induce the birthing process. I practiced my Lamaze exercises from earlier years and delivered the next day. As expected, the baby was stillborn. My heart and my soul ached with sorrow. As I was wheeled out of the delivery room, I wept.

I remained in the hospital because my leg was still paralyzed and I could not move well at all. After more tests, the doctors finally decided that a herniated disk was the cause. So at the end of a three-week stay I was discharged. The doctor sent me home with pain medication and a regimen of lots of rest, back exercises, and regular hot-pack treatments. My mother, then seventy-eight, came from Florida to help us out—my husband, our two young sons, and me. She'd planned on staying a couple of weeks. She was with us for over two months.

I've never felt as awful as I did during that time. The constant pain battered my spirit. I was frustrated, angry, sad—and I hurt all the time. Weeks passed, and I could still barely walk. I took strong medications, slept a lot, tried to do normal things as much as I could every day. I cried often from the exhaustion of constant pain. The bright spot during this time was a little gray kitten named Spooky, who had come into our household the same day that I got home from the hospital. Spooky seemed to understand my need for a comforting presence. Soft and small and warm, he curled up next to me and purred. He seemed happy and content just to be near me. He loved the sandwiches my mother brought to me, too, especially the ones with liverwurst or tuna fish salad.

I prayed a lot during this period. I've always considered prayer as conversation with God and I try to be very honest when I pray. I express doubts and fears and shortcomings as well as hopes and desires. I'm also a prayerful listener, setting aside my thoughts and quieting my mind for a time of silence. Sitting in silence helps me to bring myself into the presence of God and simply be. I'm able to relax into a deeper peace and openness than when I'm uptight with impatience or discontent. Sitting in silence is my invitation for the Spirit to guide me. It is a practice of being intentionally open to the Spirit as I listen with patience to the promptings that may come.

My prayers don't often get answered in a direct way. That is, rarely do I hear a voice in my head or get an idea that is directive. What I tend to get from being open to the Spirit is a nudge or an insight that simply comes to me and relates to something I've been concerned about or praying about. Sometimes these nudges and insights come through a book I happen to read or a conversation I have with someone. Often, I'll have an image or idea come to me as I'm waking up from a night's sleep. Other times I'll get a new perspective on a prayer-related issue while walking, listening to music, or thinking about something else entirely.

During my long weeks of recovery, I prayed fervently for healing to happen. I listened to audio tapes and read books about healing and healing prayer. Though nothing seemed to happen externally to heal me, I had an increasingly strong inner urge to *do something* toward the goal of getting better. So, with my right leg still paralyzed and my body still constantly in pain, I tried my best to function. Every day I tried to do a little more activity. I tried to walk. I tried to get dressed and go outside. After a while I was able to return to directing the weekly one-hour rehearsal of the children's choir that I had started at my church. I came home from these rehearsals stimulated but exhausted. On my journeys to and from the church on those days, I learned many things about what life is like when you can't function as you did before. I learned how hard it is to maintain a cheerful attitude when you hurt or feel completely out of energy. I learned how long it takes to cross a street when you use a cane. I learned how simple interactions with friends can be supportive and at the same time drain you of all energy. My family bore the brunt of my frustration and irritation. Friends and strangers out in the world got the benefit of my limited good will.

Those months were a spiritual challenge as well as a physical challenge for me. I mourned the loss of our baby, whose gender I'd chosen not to learn. I found out that several of my older friends had experienced something similar earlier in their lives, one with her first pregnancy. I found it oddly comforting to hear their stories. Now I felt no longer alone in knowing a mother's sadness of losing a child halfway to life. I wondered how I could have known these women well for years without knowing this soul-crunching thing about them. I realized then that there are many significant things about our lives that we don't share with others until the time feels right or there's a specific reason to share that part of our story.

Six months after my lower back injury, I was startled by what felt like a gentle but definite electric shock. It ran straight from my head down through my body and out through the big toe of my right foot. This happened on a March evening several days before a long-awaited appointment with a neurosurgeon at Yale-New Haven Medical Center. I remember thinking, "This must mean that my central nervous system is now reconnected." A sense of hope filled me. "I'm going to get better," I thought.

I kept my appointment with the neurosurgeon. He conducted some tests and asked about how I was doing. With some trepidation that he would scoff at me, I told him of my experience of the electric shock and my interpretation of it. Instead of scoffing, he took me seriously and suggested that we hold off on scheduling surgery and give my body more time to heal on its own.

With the support of a lace-up corset that had steel rods on each side of my spine plus the increased muscle strength I got from faithfully doing my daily exercises, I gradually returned to normal living. Every day I could move more easily. Over time the pain diminished to manageable levels. About six weeks after my visit to the neurosurgeon, I was able to return to the organ bench to play for two Sunday services as the substitute organist. That was a fantastic, spiritually rich day for me. I felt alive and whole once more, resurrected and victorious, ecstatic to have been returned to life.

The previous ten months had taken me on a spiritual journey through darkness and despair. I began to see that there's a strong link between spirituality and our real-life emotions. For the first time in my life, I had *consciously* grappled with the complex emotions of life and the complicated mix of opposing emotions. I had wavered between fear and courage, faith and doubt, hope and despair, anger and compassion. I had tried everything offered to me, including medieval potions from a friend who was certain of their healing power. I began to understand how people in pain will do anything to relieve it. I began to understand spirituality as the invisible and unseen resource for living life when we feel completely helpless. I began to see that our spirituality makes a difference in how we view life, how we respond to life's difficult challenges, and how we acknowledge and express joy and gratitude for the goodness and wonders of our lives. I came to understand how spirituality contributes to resilience. It gives us a lens to see ourselves and our situation anew and find meaning in it.

Kenneth Pargament writes that when we reflect on our experiences from a spiritual perspective, we can often discern deeper truths in them. "Through a spiritual lens, problems take on a different character and distinctive solutions appear: answers to seemingly unanswerable questions, support when other sources of support are unavailable, and new sources of value and significance when old dreams are no longer viable. Spirituality, then, represents a distinctive resource for living."[7]

If we haven't paid much attention to deepening our spiritual life as we've become adults, we're likely to lack the spiritual resources we'll need to be radically resilient. Our childhood understanding of spirituality is usually not adequate when we experience the kind of adversity that changes our life forever. When we search for the meaning in what has happened to us, and we search for an understanding of who we are when we can't do what we used to do, or be who we used to be, then we need spiritual resources that go deeper. We need to be able to reach out to our Higher Power and trust that we are not alone. We also need a spiritual community that can walk the journey by our side, comforting us when we need comfort, and cheering us on as we do the hard work of recovery.

Yet even when we have a strong sense of spirituality and relationship with the sacred, we can experience anguish, doubt, despair, misery, and darkness. James Hollis calls these experiences "swampland visitations" and describes how they enrich our lives and help us to grow into a mature spirituality. Encounters with these dark experiences in the spiritual framework of resilience ultimately lead to enlargement, not diminishment. "Truth be told, we wish we didn't have to grow," writes Hollis, "but life is asking more of us than that."[8]

There are often indications of the potential for spiritual growth in the emotions we feel and express. Joy, love, fear, despair, hope, anger, compassion, shame, regret, sadness, self-pity—these and other powerful emotions, common responses to the challenges of life-changing limitations, can be pathways to spiritual awareness and growth. Their spiritual dimension is their *meaning* for us—when we allow ourselves to learn from them, to see and understand ourselves in a new or deeper way.

We saw how my friend Steven engaged the resilience skills of realistic optimism and hope in his recovery from a ruptured Achilles tendon (chapter 7). But Steven also engaged with spirituality as a resilience skill—and the result was a deepening of his own sense of self. At first Steven couldn't imagine how as a very active person he could survive without being able to put weight on his leg for many months; the thought of a year of physical incapacity was more than he could tolerate. It took several days before he could reflect on his experience and begin to engage his resilience skills. He described those days as a time when he moped around the house, inwardly seething about his bad luck.

Then one morning he thought about how his accident had also brought limiting changes into his wife's life. He saw that the behaviors his feelings had generated in him were creating a burden of care for her. Suddenly he knew for certain that he didn't want her to experience this as a hard time because of how he responded to it. "That was a spiritual insight for me," he said. It broadened his worldview and transformed his self-absorbed concern into compassionate concern for another person. Usually an upbeat and positive person, Steven said he'd never before been aware of how his occasional occurrences of self-pitying behavior could have a negative effect on others.

This new awareness was very humbling and it touched him deeply. With gratitude for having seen this truth about himself, he began to think creatively about ways he could get around without putting weight on his leg. He wanted to be independent, not just for himself, but also so that he wouldn't be a burden on his wife. It was then that he remembered that he'd seen someone with a broken leg getting around on a scooter you could kneel on. He inquired about renting one and was soon getting around more easily, and much more happily, than he had thought possible.

A resilient person comes through the dark and painful times into a new and deeper sense of well-being. Though the process may be a long one, the resilient person will often say that even though there was pain and uncertainty, there was also a sense of being upheld by something greater than themselves. Sometimes, as for Steven, it was having a sudden insight that shifted his internal point of view from being focused only on himself to being concerned for how his attitude and behavior affected others. Or maybe it's a series of small things that seem to happen by coincidence—a visit from a friend, a line from a poem we happen to read, a thought or image that comes after prayer, or a book brought by a friend that's just the right story for us at the time. It can be a change in attitude or perspective that comes after a time of creative self-expression through art, writing, or music. My friend Margaret tells of how her oncology doctor simply came by and sat with her during her difficult chemo treatment one day. His gift of compassion and caring lifted her spirit and restored both her hope and her courage. Compassion itself is a spiritual value, she says. Compassion communicates to the person receiving it that they matter. It lifts them out of the depths of aloneness.

Spiritual experiences like Steven's, Margaret's, and mine are often described as "*transformative.*" Not only do they ease our tensions, neutralize our fears, and extinguish our sense of being totally alone, they change us. They make us feel more fully human, more aware of the fragility and wonder of life, and more at one with the universe and the people in it.

A resilient person will often say that their challenging experience helped them to grow emotionally and/or spiritually, or that in some way it was beneficial to their sense of self.[9] For some, the spiritual growth became evident in their increased awareness of suffering in others that led to a broader, deeper sense of compassion. For others, the sense of inner growth came in knowing that they could handle difficult and painful situations without falling apart. They felt stronger for having come through their trauma and confident in their ability to adapt to their new reality. Some say that they found God again; others, that in facing the challenges, they felt guided and supported by a loving divine presence, a higher power, for the first time. And some say that although they'd always believed in God, their faith in God was now stronger because they'd experienced God's presence in their lives.

In times of personal grief as well as in times of regional or national disaster, spiritual communities have been community gathering places. The songs and prayers become vehicles for the expression of inner confusion, chaos, and sorrow. In times of celebration, they serve as vehicles for expressing exuberance,

hope, and joy. The rituals that acknowledge birth, death, marriage, and other of life's turning points provide a container for
the multiple and often chaotic feelings that accompany the
large experiences of human life. The rituals of faith communities mark these things. They give us a way to share the experiences that are too large to hold within ourselves.

Years ago I was visiting a friend in a rural area of Penn-
sylvania. It was March, and I took a morning stroll in the
local park. I was drawn to a beautiful stream. I found myself
entranced by the flowing water as it moved smoothly along,
carrying with it some dried leaves and other woodland debris.
I found a rock to sit on and decided to simply stay a while and
be quiet in this peaceful place.

As I sat and watched the water, my attention was caught
by a cluster of dried brown oak leaves traveling down the current toward me. Just to my right I noticed a stick poking up
about eight inches out of the water. I watched as the cluster
of leaves wrapped around the stick, like pieces of paper bent
around a pencil.

As the bubbling clear water flowed around and under this
bunch of leaves, the edges of the outer leaf fluttered ever so
slightly. In a few minutes that leaf came loose and was carried
away by the current. Five minutes later another leaf was dis-
lodged, and the current carried it away also. Then a few minutes later another leaf fluttered a bit and then floated down the
stream. I imagine that if I'd stayed there several more hours, I'd
have seen all the leaves come loose and be carried away. Eventually even the stick would have been loosened from the rock
that held it and be gone.

That's a powerful image of spirituality for me. The strug-
gles that we face in our lives can cause us to get stuck in a

particular place so that emotions such as anger or hatred or resentment or defensiveness or fear cluster around our hearts like those leaves caught on the stick. If they remain there, we stay trapped in the past. Our Higher Power is like that flowing stream. But our Higher Power is not something material that we can see or touch or feel. Instead, this transcendent Spirit of the universe dwells unseen within us and around us. We grow into relationship with it by consciously and quietly bringing ourselves into its presence with an open heart.

## Some Ways to Practice Spirituality

Cultivate gratitude. By increasing our awareness of the positive things in our lives, gratitude helps us see that we're not alone, that we're part of a larger life than we sometimes can see from day to day. Gratitude is a knowing awareness that we've experienced or received something good.[10] One way to cultivate gratitude is to start a gratitude journal in which we write down five things we're grateful for each day. Another way is make a list of people who have done something for us or mean something to us and each week write a thank you note to one of the people on our list.

Cultivate compassion and kindness. Compassion occurs when we are present with care and without fear or judgment to someone who is suffering, including ourselves. When we practice compassion, we increase our ability to care—not just about individual suffering but also about social justice and the interconnectedness of all Creation. Similarly, the spiritual practice of kindness encompasses all our relationships—not just with other people but with things, animals, plants, and the earth. Kindness is both attitude and action. The attitude toward everyone and everything is one of respect. The action toward everyone and everything is one of gentleness, acceptance, and generosity. Good manners of every kind, sharing a smile with the person crossing the street in front of us, affirming the person who checks out our groceries, giving up a seat on the bus so someone else can sit down—these are just a few of the ways we can practice kindness. Practicing compassion and kindness transforms the way we see the world and respond to it by increasing our sense of interconnectedness with all things.

**Deepen your relationship with your Higher Power.** Many people find that having a sense of connection with and trust in a higher power is an important part of their spirituality. Prayer, meditation, spiritual reading, conversation with others who are on a spiritual path, and participation in a spiritual community are ways we can connect with our Higher Power. It also helps to be open to experiencing the presence of a higher power in nature, art, music, and movement. We can begin by noticing the activity of a higher power in the reality of our lives. For example, are there times when you've felt deeply connected to the universe? Are there times when intense fear has given way to a sense of calm even in the midst of danger? Are there times when you've felt alone or abandoned and someone has come to be with you? Are there times, as for Steven, when a sudden insight has led you to a new understanding of how your behaviors affect others and you see how you can become more loving or compassionate? Reflect on the presence of a higher power in your life, and pray that this power, by whatever name you call it, will show you what you need to know or understand.

**Find a spiritual community.** If you've ever had a meaningful connection with a spiritual tradition, you may want to return to your roots and be open to where the Spirit leads you. It may feel like coming home and make you eager to explore what it can mean to you now. But if you give it a try and find that it feels restrictive or not engaging, you may want to explore other spiritual paths.

If you've never had a meaningful connection to a spiritual community, or you're not interested in returning to your roots, visit faith communities that seem interesting to you. Talk with friends about their faith communities and go with them to worship or a program if you can. However, know that faith communities that follow rigid rules or promote judgmental and punitive beliefs can be obstacles to resilience. Be sure to read the small print about the values and beliefs of the traditions that interest you so that you can discern whether you want to live by the values they profess. Twelve-step programs also serve as spiritual communities for their members.

**Practice mindfulness meditation.** Spending time in silence with attention to our breathing is an ancient spiritual practice. This practice quiets our minds, slows our heart rate, and brings us into the presence of our Higher Power. Although we may perceive no immediate benefit each time we practice meditation, we'll find that our lives go better when we do it regularly. What's more, sometimes, as with prayer, we may receive a sense of direction for our life or an answer to something we've been concerned about.

Spirituality is a dynamic dimension of life. Our spirituality can change and deepen as we grow from childhood to maturity and through our later years. There are many paths to spirituality. To be radically resilient, we'll want a spirituality that will become a source of inner strength, compassion, kindness, and mercy— toward ourselves, toward others, and toward the universe.

## Summary for Chapter 9: Spirituality

### What is spirituality as a radical resilience skill?

- The way we connect with the intangible, eternal essence of life that is outside us, within us, and present in the fabric of every day.

- The dimension of life through which we make meaning of our self, our life, our world, our God, and our experiences.

- The spirituality that supports radical resilience is a holistic spirituality, one that seeks to understand the interconnectedness of all life and the oneness of all peoples through an understanding of the mind-body-spirit connection.

### What are some ways to practice spirituality?

- Cultivating gratitude.

  - Gratitude increases our awareness of the positive things in our lives, helps us see that we're not alone, that there are people in our lives—and even nature itself—that nurture us and lift our spirit.

- Cultivating compassion and kindness.

  - Compassion occurs when we are present with kindness and without fear or judgment to someone who is suffering, including ourselves.

  - When we practice compassion, we increase our ability to care—not just about individual suffering but also about social justice and the interconnectedness of all Creation.

- Deepening our relationship with our Higher Power through prayer, meditation, spiritual reading, conversation with others who are on a spiritual path, participation in a spiritual community, and through nature, art, music, and even physical activity.

- Reflecting on the presence of a higher power in our life

  - Praying that our Higher Power, by whatever name we call it, will show us what we need to know or understand.

- Finding a spiritual community.

  - It may be part of a religious tradition, a twelve-step program, a book group, or something else.

# 10

# Putting It All Together

Radical resilience is a process as well as an outcome. The process takes time—often months and sometimes years. Setbacks, plateaus, and periods of discouragement are normal parts of the process. How do we persevere when we feel so low emotionally or physically that we can't imagine how we can keep on going? How can we be resilient when we feel as though we have no control whatsoever over our situation? What do we do then?

The other nine resilience skills interact with perseverance to keep us moving forward during the down times. When we're discouraged, frustrated, or in physical or emotional pain, the skills of mindfulness, flexibility, courage, reframing, creativity, realistic optimism, hope, physical activity, and spirituality are all useful. Just thinking about ways we can use them when we're discouraged is likely to motivate us to take a step forward by enlisting one or more of the skills. For example, we saw how, in the throes of depression, Andrew (chapter 8) got himself to exercise by thinking about doing it and remembering how much better he felt afterwards.

*Mindful breathing* is always a good starting point. We can do it when we're lying down, sitting, standing, or walking. Simply focusing our attention on our breath as we inhale and exhale will relax us, reduce our inner stress, and restore our sense of having some control over our life.

*Flexibility* helps protect us from feeling powerless or guilty when we can't meet our goals for recovery. On the days we're not able to do the things that we'd planned to do, we can practice flexibility by choosing to do something we *can* do. In fact, it may be advisable to disengage from goals that now seem unattainable and replace them with goals that are easy to reach. *Realistic optimism* is the skill we use to assess and replace our goals; *hope* is the skill we use to identify small steps that will get us to the new goal. Adjusting our goals is not a sign of failure to persevere; it's an indicator of our ability to self-regulate by adapting appropriately to our circumstances.

*Courage*, especially the courage to be vulnerable, comes into play in times of discouragement. We engage our courage in several ways: through a conscious intention to move forward the best way we can; by *connecting with our Higher Power* for strength and spiritual sustenance; by engaging in whatever *physical activity* is possible for us; and by engaging in *creative expression*, either through a kind of play or practice we already enjoy or one that is new to us.

*Reframing* is helpful for moving through a setback, plateau, or time of discouragement. We can reframe by writing our thoughts and feelings in a notebook or journal and reflecting on them. Sometimes a conversation with someone else who is hurting will help us reframe our own situation. Prayer and meditation are *spiritual practices* that help us reframe by giving us a broader lens through which to see ourselves and our situation. Reframing helps us to see that we can let go of wishing that we could control our situation and instead improve the one thing we can control—our response to it.

Reframing was essential in helping my friend Frances regain her sense of self when an unhealed foot injury turned her temporary stay in a nursing home into a permanent one. Frances was a friendly, outgoing person in her early eighties. When she fell and injured her foot, she agreed to go to the nursing home for rehabilitation with the understanding that she would soon be able to return to her apartment. However, she learned that her foot would never heal well enough for her to return home, and for weeks after, Frances felt depressed and despondent. She didn't want to live any longer in this condition.

One afternoon, she overheard a nurse loudly berating an aide who was one of Frances' helpers. Frances was shocked and upset because the aide was a gentle and kind person, not deserving of such an arrogant, public rebuke. Frances began to see life in the nursing home in a new way. She saw the nursing home as a community made up of staff and residents. She was part of this community. Frances soon had a new vision for her life there—she saw that she could be a support person for all the caregivers who helped her. She decided that every time she received competent help or a check-in visit, she would acknowledge the person's effort and express her appreciation for what they did. After a while, Frances noticed that staff came more frequently to check on her and offer assistance. She enjoyed their visits. Frances regained meaning and purpose for her life and she was happy. She felt like herself again.

About a month later, the director of nurses in the nursing home visited Frances. She told Frances that she'd noticed an improvement in staff morale, but she didn't know why until she heard the aides talking about how they liked checking in on Frances and helping her if she needed anything. They said that whenever they went to see Frances, they experienced a few minutes of peace in their busy day. Frances was pleased. She began to think of small things she could do to improve the quality of life for the residents too.

It usually takes a long time to recover from an adverse life event. The things that happen that cause our life to change in an instant require vast amounts of emotional, spiritual, and physical attention throughout their long duration. That's why radical resilience is a process as well as a result. The process is to use the skills as best we can, whenever we can, to move forward—sometimes inch by inch—toward making life better.

The goal for radical resilience—the result we want—is that when we've recovered emotionally, physically, and spiritually from a life-changing adversity, we have a restored sense of self. We don't forget that the adversity happened, but we don't continue to feel diminished or freshly hurt by it. Instead, as we remember and reflect on it, we often realize that we've gained new understanding about ourselves from it. We're not glad that it happened, but we've grown in positive ways because of it. We feel grateful for our life and we're ready to live again as fully as we can.

# Acknowledgments

I am grateful to the people whose stories are shared in this book. Some stories have their source in newspapers or memoirs, some are from evidence-based research, some are from people I've known personally, and others are from my own life and experience. In most cases I've changed the names to preserve privacy; the people I've identified as friends or family have given me their permission to do so.

I acknowledge with gratitude Richard Schulz, PhD, who years ago encouraged me to apply for the research assistant position at the Institute on Aging at Portland State University, Portland, Oregon, which led to my interest in resilience and all other aspects of living well and aging well, and to Judy Rau, PhD, and Ann Williams, PhD, who accepted me as a colleague and shared with me the management of their research projects.

I am also grateful to the following people, who in various ways helped me in the writing and publication of this book: Stephen Scannell, Marian Hodges, Bev Hoeffer, Sarah Rowley, Holly Berman, Margaret Martin, Sue Snyder, Andrew Scannell, John Scannell, Arlys Fischer, Patti Evans, Susan Long, Amy Valentine, Lynda Garner, Mary Tipton, Bishop Greg Rickel, Sharon Baggett, Brendan Barnicle, Bob and Ann Williams, Stephanie Oliver, Catherine Markin, members of my writing group, Jill Kelly, and Amy Livingstone. My thanks also go to the numerous unnamed people who have expressed enthusiasm about this project and have cheered me on along the way.

Alice Updike Scannell
September 22, 2017

# Resources

The following books and internet sources are ones that I've found helpful as I've explored radical resilience. The first two books are general—they speak to self-awareness and communication skills, two important foundations for radical resilience. The resources that relate to the specific resilience skills in this book are shown under each chapter title. The last set is a list of compelling memoirs and stories I've read that illustrate radical resilience.

Patterson, Kerry, Joseph Grenny, Ron McMillan, and Al Switzler. *Crucial Conversations: Tools for Talking When Stakes Are High.* New York: McGraw Hill Education, 2012.

Excellent strategies that teach how to have safe, clear, meaningful dialogue when stress, disagreement, and/or strong emotions are present in the conversation's participants. We can learn ways to improve our communication in all of life's circumstances. It is particularly helpful in showing us how to use the skills I discuss in my own book, such as speaking with courage (chapter 3) and self-awareness (chapter 1); being flexible in our approach to problem-solving conversations (chapter 4); listening well to others in the conversation and reframing our attitudes when emotions run high (chapter 5); and paying attention to the realities of our situation (chapter 7). The approaches to conversation that are successful are mindful approaches, and so this book also enhances the material in chapter 2.

Robinson, Ken. *Finding Your Element: How to Discover Your Talents and Passions and Transform Your Life.* New York: Penguin Books, 2013.

An easy-to-read guide to self-discovery. Radical resilience requires that we have good understanding of who we are, what we love, and what our attitudes are. This book is a winner at helping us ask the right questions and do the reflections that lead to living a more fulfilling life.

## Chapter 1: Radical Resilience

Reich, John W., Alex J. Zautra, and John S. Hall, eds. *Handbook of Adult Resilience*. New York: Guilford Press.

A comprehensive handbook that includes scholarly chapters on theory, research, and practice in the field of resilience study. It features interventions and initiatives for adults with posttraumatic stress disorder and other psychological disorders and individuals with chronic illness. It also includes sections on resilience across the lifespan, social dimensions of resilience, organizational and public policy dimensions of resilience, and ethnic and cultural dimensions of resilience.

Reivich Karen and Andrew Shatte. *The Resilience Factor: 7 Keys to Finding Your Inner Strength and Overcoming Life's Hurdles*. New York: Harmony Books, 2002.

Find helpful chapters about applying resilience skills in different life arenas: marriage and long-term relationships, parenting, and work.

Sandberg, Sheryl and Adam Grant. *Option B: Facing Adversity, Building Resilience, and Finding Joy*. New York: Borzoi Books/A. A. Knopf, 2017.

Sandberg's experience of deep grief after the sudden death of her forty-seven-year-old husband Dave, and the insights about resilience that she gained as she worked through her grief, are the focus of this book. But Sandberg and Grant also explore the stories of others who have overcome hardships and rebounded from life-shattering experiences. Sandberg is a business leader, philanthropist, and the CEO of Facebook. She has established a nonprofit organization, OptionB.org, to help people build resilience and find meaning in the face of adversity.

Schlossberg, Nancy K. *Revitalizing Your Retirement: Reshaping Your Identity, Relationships, and Purpose*. Washington, DC: American Psychological Association, 2009.

The best book about resilience in retirement that I have found. Schlossberg draws on the latest research and theory, as well as in-person interviews, to provide a variety of pathways for creating a meaningful life in retirement. Her insights and compelling stories help us see how we can make the most of our retirement years.

Southwick, Steven M. and Dennis S. Charney. *Resilience: The Science of Mastering Life's Greatest Challenges.* Cambridge: Cambridge University Press, 2012.

Helpful examples of resilience in the context of post-traumatic stress disorder, especially for prisoners of war and other wartime experiences. The authors interviewed Vietnam POWs, Special Forces instructors, and civilians who had experienced severe psychological traumas in childhood, adolescence, or early adulthood. The chapters on social support (6) and role models (7) illustrate the value of social support as an important element in our capacity to be resilient.

## Chapter 2: Mindfulness

Goldstein, Elisha. *The Now Effect: How a Mindful Moment Can Change the Rest of Your Life.* New York: Atria/Simon & Schuster, 2012.

I like the approach to mindfulness practice that Goldstein suggests in this book—that we treat it as a "playful discipline." That is, we commit ourselves to following through with the practice of mindfulness by setting aside our judgment, being open to new experiences, and welcoming what we find. And since we're likely to fall off the track from time to time, we're to treat ourselves with "lightness and kindness," as we gently guide ourselves back to the practice. Goldstein's style of writing is clear, engaging, and easy to read.

———— and Bob Stahl. *MBSR Every Day: Daily Practices from the Heart of Mindfulness-Based Stress Reduction.* Oakland, CA: New Harbinger Publications, 2015.

Short chapters make this small book easy to use. A couple of pages on the topic, followed by a how-to suggestion titled "Just Do It!" is all we need to learn and practice these mindfulness-based stress reduction techniques.

Kabat-Zinn, Jon. *Full Catastrophe Living: Using the Wisdom of Your Body and Mind to Face Stress, Pain, and Illness.* New York: Bantam, 2013.

Known as one of the great classics of mind/body medicine, this is the most comprehensive work on mindfulness and its role in bringing us to peace and wholeness. In the introduction to this revised and updated edition, Kabat-Zinn noted that although the updating was done to incorporate the body of scientific evidence of the effects of mindfulness on health and well-being that had grown since the first edition twenty-five years earlier, ". . . the book remains what it was intended to be from the start—a practical guide to commonsensical ways in which to cultivate mindfulness and its deeply optimistic and transformative view of human nature."

Langer, Ellen J. *Mindfulness.* Reading, MA: Addison-Wesley, 1989.

Ellen Langer's work was my introduction to the concept of mindfulness many years ago. She clarifies mindfulness by contrasting it to mindlessness and then describes how mindfulness works. Chapters on mindful aging, creative uncertainty, mindfulness on the job, and mindfulness and health provide useful insights into how we can be mindful in all the arenas of our life. Langer has since written books about mindful learning and becoming an artist through mindful creativity.

## Chapter 3: Courage and Perseverance

Brown, Brené. *The Gifts of Imperfection: Let Go of Who You Think You're Supposed to Be and Embrace Who You Are.* Center City, MN: Hazelden Publishing, 2010.

Brown identifies courage, compassion, and connection as the gifts of imperfection. She presents ten guideposts to assist readers in letting go of assumptions about ourselves that keep us from wholehearted living. Her research on vulnerability, courage, worthiness, and shame has helped many overcome their sense of unworthiness and fear of failure and instead move forward in their lives with courage and compassion.

———. *Daring Greatly: How the Courage to Be Vulnerable Transforms the Way We Live, Love, Parent, and Lead.* New York: Avery/Penguin Random House, 2012.

Brown defines vulnerability as "uncertainty, risk, and emotional exposure." She explains how vulnerability is not only crucial for resilience, it is also at the heart of our ability to build strong relationships. She gives many examples of how to be vulnerable without being weak and suggests that without the ability to be vulnerable, we're distancing ourselves from the experiences that bring purpose and meaning to our lives.

Duckworth, Angela. *Grit: The Power of Passion and Perseverance.* New York: Scribner/Simon & Schuster, 2016.

In a mix of many stories about how *grit* leads to accomplishment of goals at least as many times, if not more, than *talent* or a high *IQ*, Duckworth shows us how to take failure in stride and keep on keeping on toward our goals.

## Chapter 4: Flexibility

Southwick, Steven and Dennis Charney. "Cognitive and Emotional Flexibility" chap. 10 in *Resilience: The Science of Mastering Life's Greatest Challenge.* Cambridge: Cambridge University Press, 2012.

The authors discuss two types of flexibility that are practiced by people who are resilient: cognitive flexibility—the way we think about things—and emotional flexibility—the way we react emotionally to stress. People who are resilient are flexible in the way they cope with stress or change; they use more than one coping style. Characteristics of both types of flexibility are presented.

## Chapter 5: Reframing

Adams, Marilee. *Change Your Questions, Change Your Life: 10 Powerful Tools for Life and Work. 2nd ed.* San Francisco: Berrett-Koehler, 2009.

I love this book. The concept of *"judger"* and *"learner"* mindsets changed how I look at—and respond to—so many things in my life that I can't even count them. I'm not a pessimist, but I usually see the downside of ideas and happenings before I see the positive side. Thanks to Adams' book, I've learned to pay attention to my mindset and identify my mindset—am I in *judger* or in *learner mode*? If I'm in a *judger mindset*, I take a step back, reframe my attitude, and approach my response as a *learner* mindset. That shift makes a big difference in how things progress—and how I feel about them. Adams has since written a book for teachers on how to use these tools to ignite the love of learning in their students: *Teaching That Changes Lives: 12 Mindset Tools for Igniting the Love of Learning* (San Francisco: Berrett-Koehler Publishers, 2013).

Dweck, Carol. *Mindset: The New Psychology of Success*. New York: Random House, 2006.

As a young researcher, Dweck started out with the intention of understanding how people cope with failures. It wasn't long before she discovered that people differ in how they look at life and its challenges. Some people operate from the belief that our personal traits are fixed—we're either smart or we're not, talented or we're not, athletic or we're not. For these people, failure is bad—it implies that they have failed as a person. Dweck identified these people as having a "*fixed mindset.*" Other people operate from the belief that regardless of how we start off, we can change and grow. They believe that it's not possible to foresee what we can accomplish if we keep working at what we want to do. For these people, failure, though it may be temporarily discouraging, is viewed as an opportunity to learn and grow. Dweck identifies people who see failure as an opportunity to learn as having a "*growth mindset.*" This book gives us a different perspective on reframing, so that we see can see the opportunities for growth in our experiences of failure and adversity.

Southwick, Steven and Dennis Charney. "Cognitive and Emotional Flexibility" chap. 10 in *Resilience: The Science of Mastering Life's Greatest Challenge*. Cambridge: Cambridge University Press, 2012.

A presentation of cognitive reappraisal as a component of flexibility. Cognitive reappraisal is one way that we can reframe a situation and see it differently. The authors present findings from neuroscience that show how cognitive reappraisal affects our brain. They identify acceptance, gratitude, and humor as ways we can use to reappraise situations and events.

## Chapter 6: Creativity

Galindo, Javy W. *The Power of Thinking Differently: An Imaginative Guide to Creativity, Change, and the Discovery of New Ideas. 2nd ed.* Los Altos, CA: Hyena Press, 2011.

Galindo explores creative thinking through the rational lens of psychology and neuroscience as well as through the imaginative lens of analogy, fable, jokes, and puzzles. He likens the creative process to a journey—not a linear one but one in which we are likely to jump back and forth between various stages of the creative process—from tinkering with new ideas to finding insights, back to tinkering, then taking the insights further into decisions and development of the ideas, for example. This engaging book looks at creative approaches found in art, science, business, everyday living, the author's experiences, and more.

Kelly, Jill and Bridget Benton. *Sober Play: Using Creativity for a More Joyful Recovery.* Portland, OR: 3 Cats Publishing, 2013.

A book for anyone who wants to find their way into creative self-expression. Although the structure is based on the twelve-step model of recovery from addictive behaviors, the premise of the book is that creativity is a natural part of who we are as human beings. The authors share their experience of working and playing with close to two dozen forms of creative self-expression from fiber arts to woodworking. They make a broad range of suggestions for how we can get started with the ones that appeal to us. And they remind us that the only way to fail at artmaking of any kind is to not do it.

Michalko, Michael. *Thinkertoys: A Handbook of Creative-Thinking Techniques.* Berkley: Ten Speed Press/Crown Publishing, 2006.

Michalko is adept at inspiring us to overcome our fears, uncertainties, and doubts (he calls them our FUDS) and to jump right into fun exercises that challenge our minds and foster creative thinking. This book includes hints, tricks, tips, tales, and puzzles that open our minds to a multitude of innovative solutions to all kinds of everyday problems.

## Chapter 7: Realistic Optimism and Hope

Lyubomirsky, Sonja. *The How of Happiness: A Scientific Approach to Getting the Life You Want.* New York: Penguin Books, 2007.

Lyubomirsky is a professor of psychology at the University of California, Riverside. This carefully researched and readable book shows that there are connections between several of the resilience skills and happiness. These include cultivating optimism, nurturing social relationships, taking care of your soul (spirituality), and taking care of your body (physical activity).

Seligman, Martin E.P. *Learned Optimism: How to Change Your Mind and Your Life*, 2nd ed. New York: Free Press, 1998.

> Seligman draws on more than twenty years of clinical research to demonstrate how optimism enhances our quality of life and how anyone can learn to practice it. He explains how we can recognize if our *explanatory style* is pessimistic or optimistic, and shows us how to approach life with "flexible optimism."

### Chapter 8: Physical Activity

Duhigg, Charles. *The Power of Habit: Why We Do What We Do in Life and Business.* New York: Random House, 2014.

> Duhigg's exploration of how habits are formed and how we can change them has relevance for all resilience skills. Although this book first turned me around about exercise, it has taught me how to analyze and change other habits that hinder my capacity for resilience. Duhigg is a great storyteller; this is a fascinating as well as very helpful read.

US National Institute on Aging. *Exercise & Physical Activity: Your Everyday Guide from the National Institute on Aging.* 2009.

> An excellent guide to exercise and physical activity for senior adults. It's available online from the National Institute on Aging, a branch of the National Institutes on Health. You can download it as a PDF file, order a free printed copy, and order a free accompanying DVD at: *https://order.nia.nih.gov/publication/exercise-physical-activity-your-everyday-guide-from-the-national-institute-on-aging*

Another good source of information about exercise and physical activity for people of all ages is the Australian Department of Health website: *http://www.health.gov.au/internet/main/publishing.nsf/content/health-pubhlth-strateg-phys-act-guidelines*

The following website, also from the Australian Department of Health, is specific to physical activity and sedentary behavior: *http://www.health.gov.au/paguidelines*

### Chapter 9: Spirituality

Brussat, Frederick and Mary Ann. *Spiritual Rx: Prescriptions for Living a Meaningful Life.* New York: Hyperion, 2000.

A practical guide for beginner and seasoned practitioner alike. Drawing from a wide range of spiritual writers and traditions, the authors have written an invaluable guide to spiritual practices and resources. The following is from their introduction:

> Whether you are affiliated with one of the world's religions or are more comfortable with a free-floating spirituality, whether you are conservative or liberal, experienced or just beginning, there is room for you on the common ground of practice. A chief characteristic of the path of practice is its inclusivity. Everyone belongs.

Their chapter, "Finding Your Prescription of Practices," guides readers in how to put together a good set of spiritual practices that fits their own interests and needs. This chapter explains that there are many ways to approach spiritual practice and then describes them in enough detail that we can discern which approaches we might want to try first.

Each of the thirty-seven short chapters that present a spiritual practice includes a variety of ways we can approach that practice. The chapters also include resources for further exploration of the practice include fiction, poetry, children's books, videos or spoken-word audio, art, and music. The practices are presented alphabetically, from "*Attention*" through "*Zeal*." A sampling of the practices includes "*Being Present*," "*Compassion*," "*Grace*," "*Hospitality*," "*Imagination*," "*Transformation*," "*Vision*," "*Wonder*," and "*Yearning*."

Emmons, Robert. *Thanks! How New Science of Gratitude Can Make You Happier*. Boston: Houghton Mifflin Harcourt, 2007.

Based on a solid and growing body of research, and drawing from the writings of philosophers, novelists, and theologians, and ancient wisdom, Emmons shows that the cultivation of gratitude can immensely improve our quality of life. His thorough exploration of gratitude includes chapters on gratitude and the human spirit, gratitude in trying times, and obstacles to grateful living. In the final chapter he presents ten ways to build the practice of gratitude into our lives.

Fox, Matthew. *Creation Spirituality: Liberating Gifts for the Peoples of the Earth*. New York: HarperCollins, 1991.

I find Fox's creation-centered spirituality to be a compelling spirituality for radical resilience because it understands that our experience of the divine will be found through more than one spiritual path. We can experience God in the awe, wonder, and mystery of nature and of all beings (path 1). We can experience God in darkness and nothingness, in silence and emptying, in letting go and letting be, and in pain and suffering (path 2). We can experience God in our creativity, our generativity, and or imaginative output (path 3). And, we can experience God in the combatting of injustice, the relief of suffering, the struggle for balance in society and history, and the celebration that happens when persons struggling for justice and trying to live in mutuality come together to praise and give thanks for the gift of being, and of being together (path 4). Fox's spirituality resonates with many people who seek a broad spirituality that encompasses social justice, nonviolence, and living in harmony with the world.

Langford Heron, Lisa and Brian. *7 Steps to Finding Your Spiritual Life.* Lincoln, NE: iUniverse Inc., 2005.

This helpful workbook introduces a way of talking about spirituality that is accessible to anyone. It identifies and defines seven basic domains or areas of spiritual life, helps the reader explore each one, and offers a process of discovery through which readers can find a meaningful spiritual path for their life.

Ozment, Katherine. *Grace without God: The Search for Meaning, Purpose, and Belonging in a Secular Age.* New York: HarperCollins, 2016.

The author, an award-winning journalist, explores the values of religious traditions and suggests ways that nonreligious Americans can create their own traditions and communities in a secular age.

The section on "Charting Your Own Path," in the *Resources for Readers* chapter, includes suggestions on how to reflect on your own experience with the meaningful aspects of life that are central to religious traditions: community and belonging, rituals, meaning and purpose, identity, and morality and values.

## Memoirs and Other Books That Illustrate Radical Resilience

Bauby, Jean-Dominique. *The Diving Bell and the Butterfly: A Memoir of Life in Death.* Paris: Éditions Robert Laffont, 1997.

"A wistful, poetic, ironic and whimsically affirmative testament by a man who refused to die in spirit." *The New York Times.*

Bolte Taylor, Jill. *My Stroke of Insight: A Brain Scientist's Personal Journey.* New York: Penguin Books, 2006.

This is not only the remarkable story of recovery from stroke—it's a story of discovering the physiology of thoughts and feelings, and of consciousness as well.

Cohen, Richard M. *Blindsided: Lifting a Life above Illness.* New York: HarperCollins, 2004.

A story of living with multiple sclerosis and colon cancer.

———. *Strong at the Broken Places: Voices of Illness, a Chorus of Hope.* New York: HarperCollins, 2008.

Cohen tells the remarkable stories of five ordinary people who are trapped in the world of serious chronic illness: ALS, non-Hodgkin's lymphoma, Crohn's disease, muscular dystrophy, and bipolar disorder.

Saks, Elyn R. *The Center Cannot Hold: My Journey through Madness.* New York: Hyperion, 2007.

The author, a professor of law, psychology, psychiatry and the behavioral sciences at the University of Southern California Law School, has suffered from schizophrenia for most of her life. This book is an eloquent and moving story of her life that includes the difficult obstacles she's had to overcome.

Sanford, Matthew. *Waking: A Memoir of Trauma and Transcendence.* New York: Rodale, 2006.

A story of living with a body that is paralyzed from the chest down, the result of an auto accident at age thirteen.

# Notes

## Introduction

1. Steven M. Southwick and Dennis S. Charney, *Resilience: The Science of Mastering Life's Greatest Challenges* (Cambridge: Cambridge University Press, 2012). See also John W. Reich, Alex J. Zautra, and John S. Hall, eds. *Handbook of Adult Resilience* (New York: Guilford Press).

## Chapter 1: Radical Resilience

1. Anne Saker, "Portland's Jan Schumacher Rebuilds Her Life, Minus Her Fingers," *The Oregonian*, September 21, 2011, *https://www.oregonlive.com/portland/2011/09/portland_woman_rebuilds_her_li.html*

2. Luigi Ferucci, "The Baltimore Longitudinal Study of Aging (BLSA): A 50-Year-Long Journey and Plans for the Future," *Journal of Gerontology: Medical Sciences* 63, no. 12 (2008): 1416–19.

3. Richard Boyatzis and Annie McKee, *Resonant Leadership: Renewing Yourself and Connecting with Others Through Mindfulness, Hope, and Compassion.* (Boston: Harvard Business Press, 2005). For other examples, see Daniel H. Pink, *Drive: The Surprising Truth about What Motivates Us* (New York: Riverview, 2009); Angela Duckworth, *Grit: The Power of Passion and Perseverance* (New York: Scribner, 2016); Chip and Daniel Heath, *Switch: How to Change Things When Change is Hard* (New York: Broadway, 2010).

## Chapter 2: Mindfulness

1. Connie J. G. Gersick and J. Richard Hackman, "Habitual Routines in Task-Performing Groups," *Organizational Behavior and Human Decisions Processes* 47, no. 1 (1990): 65–97.

2. Ellen Langer, *Mindfulness* (Reading, MA: Addison-Wesley, 1989), 4.

3. Gersick and Hackman, 65–97

4. Boyatzis and McKee, 8.

5. Olivia Hoblitzelle, *Ten Thousand Joys and Ten Thousand Sorrows: A Couple's Journey through Alzheimer's* (New York: Jeremy P. Tarcher/Penguin Group, 2010).

6. Hoblitzelle, 20–21.

7. Hoblitzelle, 229.

8. Daphne M. Davis and Jeffrey A. Hayes, "What are the Benefits of Mindfulness? A Practice Review of Psychotherapy-Related Research," *Psychotherapy* 48, no. 2 (2011): 198–208.

9. Paul Grossman, Ludger Niemann, Stefan Schmidt, and Harald Walach, "Mindfulness-Based Stress Reduction and Health Benefits: A Meta-Analysis," *Journal of Psychosomatic Research*, 57, no. 1 (2004): 35–43.

10. Linda Carlson, "Mindfulness-Based Interventions for Physical Conditions: A Narrative Review Evaluating Levels of Evidence." *ISRN Psychiatry* (2012), doi:10.5402/2012/651583

11. Jon Kabat-Zinn, *Full Catastrophe Living: Using the Wisdom of Your Body and Mind to Face Stress, Pain, and Illness* (New York: Bantam, 2013), 158.

12. Elisha Goldstein and Bob Stahl, *MBSR Every Day: Daily Practices from the Heart of Mindfulness-Based Stress Reduction* (Oakland, CA: New Harbinger, 2015), 54–73.

## Chapter 3: Courage and Perseverance

1. Brené Brown, *Daring Greatly* (New York: Penguin, 2012).

2. Debra Bournes, "Having Courage: A Lived Experience of Human Becoming," *Nursing Science Quarterly*, 15, no. 3 (2002): 225.

3. Bournes, 220–29.

4. Bournes, 223.

5. Edwin Catmull with Amy Wallace, *Creativity, Inc.: Overcoming the Unseen Forces That Stand in the Way of True Inspiration* (New York: Random House, 2014), 108–10.

6. Catmull, 109.

7. Jill Bolte Taylor, *My Stroke of Insight: A Brain Scientist's Personal Journey* (New York: Penguin/Viking, 2006).

8. Taylor, 127.

## Chapter 4: Flexibility

1. Jane Kallir and Roger Cardinal, *Grandma Moses in the 21st Century*. (New Haven, CT: Yale University Press, 2001), 8. Details of her life are from Wikipedia.

2. Isaac Galetzer-Levy, Charles L. Burton, and George A. Bonanno, "Coping Flexibility, Potentially Traumatic Life Events and Resilience: A Prospective Study of College Student Adjustment," *Journal of Social and Clinical Psychology* 31, no. 6 (2012): 542–67, doi: 10.1521/scp.2012.3.1.6.542. See also George A. Bonanno, Anthony Papa, Kathleen Lalande, Maren Westphal, and Karin Coifman, "The Ability to Both Enhance and Suppress Emotional Expression Predicts Long-Term Adjustment," *Psychological Science* 15, no. 7 (2004): 482–87.

3. Al Siebert, *The Survivor Personality: Why Some People are Stronger, Smarter, and More Skillful at Handling Life's Difficulties . . . and How You Can Be, Too* (New York: Berkley, 1996), 25–37.

4. Siebert, 27.

5. Bonanno, et al.

6. Erica Jong, "Blood and Guts: The Tricky Problem of Being a Woman Writer in the Late Twentieth Century," in *The Writer on Her Work*, ed. Janet Sternberg (New York: W. W. Norton, 1980), 169–79.

7. Area Agencies on Aging (AAAs) are local aging programs that provide information and services on a range of assistance for older adults and those who care for them. By contacting your local agency, you get access to critical information including available services in your area; mobility assistance programs, meal plans and housing; assistance in gaining access to services; individual counseling, support groups, and caregiver training; respite care; and supplemental services, on a limited basis. For more information, contact the National Association of Area Agencies on Aging, *https://www.n4a.org/*

## Chapter 5: Reframing

1. Robert Coles, *The Call of Stories: Teaching and the Moral Imagination* (Boston: Houghton Mifflin, 1989), 31–39.

2. Coles, 36.

3. Coles, 39.

4. Marilee Adams, *Change Your Questions, Change Your Life: 10 Powerful Tools for Life and Work*, 2nd ed. (San Francisco: Berrett-Koehler, 2009).

5. Molly Mettler and Donald W. Kemper, *Healthwise for Life: Medical Self-Care for Healthy Aging* (Boise: Healthwise, 1992), 310.

## Chapter 6: Creativity

1. Gene D. Cohen, *The Creative Age: Awakening Human Potential in the Second Half of Life* (New York: HarperCollins, 2000), 13.

2. "George de Mestral: Velcro Inventor," website for Smithsonian Institution's Lemelson Center for the Study of Invention and Innovation, April 15, 2014. *https://invention.si.edu/george-de-mestral-velcro-inventor*

3. Shaun McNiff, *Art Heals: How Creativity Cures the Soul.* (Boston: Shambhala, 2004), flyleaf.

4. Mater Mea, "Kathe LeBeau, Kidney Disease Survivor, Goes to Clown College after Life-Threatening Diagnosis," *The Huffington Post*, February 20, 2013. *https://www.huffpost.com/entry/kathe-lebeau-clown-college-kidney-disease_n_2646812*

5. Mater Mea, "Kathe LeBeau."

6. Abigail Sims, "Creative Expression," Joyful Heart Foundation, n.d. *http://www.joyfulheartfoundation.org/reunion/creative-expression*

7. Sims, "Creative Expression."

8. Frances Reynolds and Bella Vivat, "Narratives of Art-Making in Chronic Fatigue Syndrome/Myalgic Encephalomyelitis: Three Case Studies," *Arts in Psychotherapy* 33, no. 5 (2006): 435–45. All references to Julia and Grace in the narrative come from this source.

9. Jodi Bassett, "What is M. E.?" The Hummingbird Foundation for M. E. *https://www.hfme.org/whatisme.htm*

10. Sandra Siedliecki and Marion Good, "Effect of Music on Power, Pain, Depression and Disability," *Journal of Advanced Nursing* 54, no. 5, (2006): 553–62, doi:10.1111/j.1365-2648.2006.03860.x

11. Oliver Sacks, *Musicophilia: Talks of Music and the Brain* (New York: Vintage, 2008). 255–56 discusses music helping people walk again; 232–42 for helping people talk again; 247–53 for helping people with Tourette's Syndrome.

12. Sacks, 251–52.

13. Sacks, 252.

14. Ken Robinson with Lou Arnica, *The Element: How Finding Your Passion Changes Everything* (New York: Viking Penguin, 2009), 77.

15. I heard this story of Janet and Roger many years ago at a presentation by a faculty member of the School of Occupational Therapy at Pacific University in Forest Grove, Oregon. I've given them new names, but their story of how creativity can make a huge difference in people's quality of life and their interest in living made a lasting impression on me.

16. Peter Pronovost and Eric Vohr, *Safe Patients, Smart Hospitals: How One Doctor's Checklist Can Help Us Change Healthcare from the Inside Out* (New York: Hudson Street Press, 2010), 20–23.

17. Pronovost and Vohr, 113–43.

18. Ken Robinson, *Out of Our Minds: Learning to be Creative* (West Sussex, UK: Capstone, 2011), 142.

## Chapter 7: Realistic Optimism and Hope

1. Martin E. P. Seligman, *Learned Optimism: How to Change Your Mind and Your Life*, 2nd ed. (New York: Free Press, 1998), 207. See also Sonja Lyubomirsky, *The How of Happiness: A Scientific Approach to Getting the Life You Want* (New York: Penguin, 2008), 103–11.

2. Southwick and Charney, "Cognitive and Emotional Flexibility," 39. See also Margarethe Aase Schaufel, Jan Erik Nordrehaug, and Kirsti Malterud, "Hope in Action—Facing Cardiac Death: A Qualitative Study of Patients with Life-Threatening Disease," *International Journal of Qualitative Studies on Health and Well-being* 6, no. 1 (2011), doi:10.3402/qhw.v6i1.5917

3. S. L. Schneider, "In Search of Realistic Optimism: Meaning, Knowledge, and Warm Fuzziness," *American Psychologist* 56, no. 3 (2001): 250–63, http://dx.doi.org/ 10.1037/0003-66X.56.3.250

4. Al Siebert, *The Resiliency Advantage: Master Change, Thrive under Pressure, and Bounce Back from Setbacks* (San Francisco: Barrett-Koehler, 2005).

5. We saw this in the chapter on flexibility. Siebert, *The Survivor Personality*, 25–37.

6. Charles R. Snyder, *The Psychology of Hope: You Can Get There from Here* (New York: Free Press, 1994).

7. Richard M. Cohen, *Blindsided: Lifting a Life above Illness* (New York: HarperCollins, 2004).

8. Cohen, interview by Dr. Manny Alvarez, *FoxNews.com*, August 19, 2014, *https://www.foxnews.com/health/coping-with-ms-richard-m-cohens-41-year-journey*

9. Snyder, 50–54.

10. David B. Feldman and Maximilian M. Kubota, "Hope," in *Religion, Spirituality and Positive Psychology: Understanding the Psychological Fruits of Faith*, ed. Thomas G. Plante (Santa Barbara: Praeger, 2012), 55.

11. John C. Barefoot, Beverly H. Brummett, Redford B. Williams, Ilene C. Siegler, Michael J. Helms, Stephen H. Boyle, Nancy E. Clapp-Channing, and Daniel B. Mark, "Recovery Expectations and Long-Term Prognosis of Patients with Coronary Heart Disease," *Archives of Internal Medicine* 171, no. 10 (2011): 929–35, doi:10.1001/archinternmed.2011.41

12. Lyubomirsky, 111.

13. Seligman, 115.

14. Lyubomirsky, 161–62.

## Chapter 8: Physical Activity

1. Frank J. Penedo and Jason R. Dahn, "Exercise and Well-Being: A Review of Mental and Physical Health Benefits Associated with Physical Activity," *Current Opinion in Psychiatry* 18, no. 2 (2005): 189–93. See also Heidi Godman, "Regular Exercise Changes the Brain to Improve Memory, Thinking Skills," *Harvard Health Blog*, April 9, 2014, *https://www.health.harvard.edu/blog/regular-exercise-changes-brain-improve-memory-thinking-skills-201404097110*

2. Marily Opprezzo and Daniel L. Schwartz, "Give Your Ideas Some Legs: The Positive Effect of Walking on Creative Thinking," *Journal of Experimental Psychology: Learning, Memory and Cognition* 40, no. 4 (2014): 1143–52.

3. World Health Organization, "Fact Sheet on Physical Activity," February 28, 2018, *https://www.who.int/news-room/fact-sheets/detail/physical-activity*

4. James A. Levine, "Your Chair: Comfortable but Deadly," *Diabetes* 59, no. 11 (2010): 2715–16, doi:10.2337/db10-1042.

5. Seligman, *Learned Optimism,* 15. Seligman's entire definition of learned helplessness is "the giving-up reaction, the quitting response that follows from the belief that whatever you do doesn't matter."

6. J. Avorn and E. Langer, "Induced Disability in Nursing Home Patients: A Controlled Trial," Abstract. *Journal of the American Geriatrics Society* 30, no. 6 (1982): 397–400. doi.10.1111/j.1532-5415.1982.tb02839.x/full

7. Irene participated in PACE (Program of All-Inclusive Care of the Elderly), a program funded jointly by Medicare and Medicaid, which provided integrated care to frail older people who qualified for nursing home care so that they could live with family or in a community-based setting. For information about PACE go to *https:// www.medicare.gov/ your-Medicare-costs/help-paying-costs/pace/ pace.html*

8. Andrew Solomon, *The Noonday Demon: An Atlas of Depression* (New York: Scribner, 2001), 139.

9. Jason T. Newsom, Nathalie Huguet, Michael J. McCarthy, Pamela Ramage-Morin, Mark S. Kaplan, Julie Bernier, Bentson H. McFarland, Jillian Oderkirk, "Health Behavior Change Following Chronic Illness in Middle and Later Life," *The Journals of Gerontology* 67, no. 3 (2012): 279–88.

10. Bill's story was adapted from www.swimming.org and retrieved June 21, 2015 but is no longer maintained on that website.

11. Charles Duhigg, *The Power of Habit: Why We Do What We Do in Life and Business* (New York: Random House Trade Paperback, 2014), 288–98.

## Chapter 9: Spirituality

1. Some of these descriptions of spirituality are from responses sent by readers of the website www.LiveandDare.com. The author, Giovanni, included them in a blog, "Spiritual Disciplines and Development."

2. Matthew Fox, *Creation Spirituality: Liberating Gifts for the Peoples of the Earth* (New York: HarperCollins, 1991), 12.

3. Matthew Sanford, *Waking: A Memoir of Trauma and Transcendence* (New York: Rodale, 2006).

4. Sanford, 221–222.

5. David E. Vance, Mark Brennan, Comfort Enah, Glenda L. Smith, and Jaspreet Kaur, "Religion, Spirituality, and Older Adults with HIV: Critical Personal and Social Resources for an Aging Epidemic." *Clinical Interventions in Aging*, no. 6 (2011): 101–109, doi: 10.2147/CIA.S16349

6. C. M. Puchalski, "Spirituality in the Cancer Trajectory," *Annals of Oncology* 23, (2012): iii49–iii55, doi:10.1093/annonc/mds088

7. Kenneth Pargament, *Spiritually Integrated Psychotherapy: Understanding and Addressing the Sacred* (New York: Guilford, 2007), 12.

8. James Hollis, *Finding Meaning in the Second Half of Life* (New York: Gotham, 2005), 234.

9. Southwick and Charney, "Cognitive and Emotional Flexibility," 176.

10. Robert A. Emmons, *Thanks! How the New Science of Gratitude Can Make You Happier* (New York: Houghton Mifflin, 2007).